BEAUTY

— FOR —

ASHES

MESSAGES OF HOPE
AN ANTHOLOGY

DELVIA Y. BERRIAN
AND SIX MESSENGERS OF HOPE

ISBN: 978-1-7349439-7-9
Library of Congress Cataloging-in-Publication Date is available.

Project Specialist/Author Coach
Barlow Enterprises, LLC
Write Your Book Now! Visit: www.destinystatement.com
or Text 478-227-5692

Legal Disclaimer

While none of the stories in this book are fabricated, some of the names and details may have been changed to protect the privacy of the individuals mentioned. Although the author and publisher have made every effort to ensure that the information in this book was correct at time of press, the author and publisher do not assume and hereby disclaim any liability to any party for any loss, damage, or disruption caused by errors or omissions, whether such errors or omissions result from negligence, accident, or any other cause.

Ordering Information

Beauty for Ashes :Messages of Hope may be purchased in large quantities at a discount for educational, business, or sales promotional use. For more information or to request Ms. Delvia Y. Berrian, or any of the authors, as the speaker at your next event, email: beautyforashes520@gmail.com

PRAISE FOR BEAUTY FOR ASHES: MESSAGES OF HOPE

As a minister of the gospel, I am often invited to speak to groups large and small. Despite the size of the audience to whom I present, I highly value being transparent and honest with people. In fact, doing so is central to my mission. Consequently, when people approach me after I have presented and perplexedly ask, "Why are you so transparent and honest about your life?" I am often taken aback. Usually, I smile and answer, "I just say what God gives me to say." Sometimes I reply, "I really don't know!" After some soul searching, however, the answer hit me like a ton of bricks. My honest, transparent presentations are purposed to give others hope! The same is to be said about the authors of these amazing stories.

Hope is a state of mind. When I speak to others, I am granted the awesome privilege and responsibility of transforming the minds of those who listen to what I have to share. So often, I inspire them to expect positive outcomes despite the horrid and hopeless events and circumstances that burden their lives at large. Needless to say, I take great care and joy in using my gifts in this way because I understand what a powerful way this is to help and serve others!

Beauty for Ashes, Messages of Hope is a compilation of six compelling, honest, transparent true stories. The brave authors of these messages of hope offer you their cheerful optimism and positivity.

Each author shares their personal lived experiences from a deep place within that is unique to each of them. They share, in their own words, how God has changed their lives from something hopeless into something hope-filled and beautiful!

There are a number of powerful lessons within, but the overarching purpose of the book is to offer you hope. These authors' diverse experiences and contributions present the unique opportunity for readers, from all walks of life, to be enriched and made hopeful again.

Through their transparent and honest accounts, the authors of *Beauty for Ashes Messages of Hope* do a superb job of giving everyone who reads this book one of the precious gifts of all—HOPE!

Anita C. Gregory, PhD

FOREWORD

Life can be daunting, especially when you consistently feel the pressure and weight of its many trying experiences. The tests of life may have you asking serious questions like, "When will morning come for me? When will this night season end? When will the blue sky come to erase the gray that has been hovering over my life?"

Inevitably, when we learn to push forward and fight for our lives, trying times birth tremendous change. When we endure through the tears that fall from our heavy hearts, we position ourselves to birth words of wisdom that will encourage someone's soul or to pen lyrics that become the perfect song to calm someone's spiritual unrest. Even more, when we persevere through tough times and maintain hope, we birth testimonies that show others that they can make it through their storms too.

We may not like the experiences that we go through, but those tough times make us strong. The poignant stories that are written in this book are a testament to this fact. The stories of the men and women who have wrestled through storms, fought through opposition, endured hardships, and pushed through adversity will inspire you. As a matter of fact, the inspiring visionary of this anthology, Delvia Y. Berrian, is a symbol of hope, strength, endurance, courage, and fortitude. Jesus Christ is the anchor and light who brought her through all that she has experienced. Jesus Christ made her a conqueror through it all.

Ultimately, God is the deliverer, restorer, redeemer, and way-maker for us all and, like Ms. Berrian and the authors of *Beauty for Ashes: Messages of Hope*, when you read what they have shared, you can become an overcomer too! Read and learn from their stories. They felt defeated, but because of God's hand of grace now they sing an anthem of victory.

I witnessed Ms. Berrian's triumph. I know that this book will encourage those who read it to see God as the One who has the power, authority, and strength to pull them beyond the ashes and into a place in which they can recognize the beauty that is deep within them. Her story, along with the others, reveals God's truth and empower readers to rise up to see that victory is attainable.

None of us are exempt from life experiences but knowing that people just like you and me were able to triumph, stand steadfast, encourage themselves, fight back, be strong and courageous, and find the light on the other side, teaches us that we can do it too!

Let God's hand, and this book, help you through the hopeless places of your life so that you can live out your life's purpose and help others to do the same.

Reverend December Pike

CONTENTS

MESSAGE OF HOPE 1 1
   THE WALK OF LIFE 3
   TAWANDA BROOKINS

MESSAGE OF HOPE 2 17
   RELENTLESS PURSUIT 19
   LATRICE LE-ANN BOOKER

MESSAGE OF HOPE 3 41
   THE DEEP END OF THE OCEAN............................. 43
   STACI LA`MARR MORGAN

MESSAGE OF HOPE 4 57
   IT ALL WORKS 59
   JENNELL MADDOX

MESSAGE OF HOPE 5 75
   MY PAST GAVE ME A PATH TO THE FUTURE...................... 77
   KELLI M. GRAY

MESSAGE OF HOPE 6 97
   INCARCERATION SAVED ME 99
   KEENAN BISHOP

MESSAGE OF HOPE 7 111
   ET TU, BRUTE?...113
   DELVIA Y. BERRIAN

MESSAGE OF HOPE

MESSAGE OF HOPE

THE WALK OF LIFE
TAWANDA BROOKINS

Good things are coming down the road. Just don't stop walking.
— Robert Warren Painter, Jr.

During my stay in prison, I had developed a habit of walking. Being behind those walls will make you enjoy and appreciate the smaller things in life and not take anything for granted. The best part of my day is when it was time for Yard Move. I would wait in anticipation to hear the correctional officer yell, "Yard!" I could not get there fast enough, to get peace of mind, the smell of fresh air. And not just any air, but mountain air.

I was housed at SCI Cambridge Springs, a women's correctional facility near Lake Erie, located six hours away from home (Philadelphia). The air up there was different from what I was used to back home; much cleaner. The clouds were amazing, the sunrise and sunset were stunning, the trees outside of the gates were beautiful, and the winter months were extremely cold. I remember one day, it must have been the coldest and iciest day, and I was the only one outside walking the track besides the guard, and he was not happy about being out there, either. I did not care; I wanted my recreation time and my piece of mind. The track had to have at least a foot of ice on top of it, and it was slippery and frigid outside. But that did not stop me from enjoying nature's beauty.

That was how I began to enjoy walking. I found solace in walking. Being in a dark place away from your loved ones can really mess with your mental and emotional state, so I had to find something that would take away the mental and emotional pain. Not only did walking help me mentally and emotionally, but I had also started to notice that I was losing weight. So walking and working out became a lifestyle for me. A lifestyle that I have continued to this very day.

Another benefit of walking is that I have time to think and observe. I notice a lot of things while walking, as opposed to driving. The two most memorable times of me walking were when I walked out of those prison gates and when I went for my daily routine of walking and stumbled across a beauty salon.

WALK OF FREEDOM

I woke around 6:30 AM. The morning news was on the television in the common area and they were bringing in breakfast. Breakfast was a cold and hard donut, cereal, fruit, and milk, and I ate the fruit and cereal. The food and commissary at Montgomery County Correctional Facility were horrible, though the food and commissary upstate was much better. I was transported from SCI Cambridge Springs back to MCCF because I had won my appeal and had to go back to court. My conviction was overturned and I was waiting to be released. It was a long process, but I had to wait for SCI Cambridge Springs to sign a release form and send it to MCCF.

I knew that I was being released, but I did not know when. My anxiety was at an all-time high. So, to release some of that anxiety,

I asked to go outside and walk. MCCF does not have a yard or a track, but a space with four brick walls that is about two hundred square feet. All the pods must share that space, and it was so small that most ladies would not bother to go outside. Not me; I needed to release that anxiety, get some air, and walk.

I was outside by myself for several hours, walking and doing pushups, squats, lounges, jumping jacks, and crunches; playing wall ball; laying on the concrete gazing at the sky, and even giving myself a pedicure (rubbing my feet against the wall), which was a small part of the beauty regime. Prison can make you become highly creative. I had repeated those activities over and over, and stopped counting after the fifth or sixth time. Finally, the guard came and escorted me back to the pod. They had already changed shifts by then.

I had missed lunch, but I did not mind because I knew I was not going to eat it anyway. Once I arrived back onto the pod, I had a cup of water and got into the shower. It was around 3:00PM. I had attempted to call my cousin Tyana, like I always did. She was my ride or die, but when I dialed her number and entered my code, it said that my funds were unavailable.

That was when I knew the ball was rolling for me to get out of there. She was the one calling SCI Cambridge Springs and MCCF to have them sign my release papers. When I say she was calling them, I mean she was calling them like they owed her money, and my cousin did not play about her paper. I then went into the cell and started gathering my things. I gave away all my food from commissary and most of my belongings, except for my pictures and important documents. I was still waiting to be released when it was time for Count, so we were locked down until Count was over. I was in the cell doing pushups and sit-ups to release some the anxiety about fifteen minutes after Count. I had noticed an unfamiliar male in the bubble (the place where the guards were stationed) and when he entered the pod, I had a feeling that he was coming for me. I just knew it.

And he was.

I had yelled, "Are you here for me?!"

The only thing I remember him saying was, "Are you Tawanda Brookins?"

I screamed with excitement, "Yes, I am her!"

"Someone really loves you, and this is your lucky day! Pack your things; you are being released!" he said with a smile on his face.

I said, "It was my cousin, Tyana, right?"

He said, "Yep! That is why I wanted to come here personally, to meet you and tell you face to face."

I was released about an hour later, and the feeling of walking out through that metal door and into the sallyport was indescribable. I could not get out there fast enough. I was so overjoyed that I had ran up toward the gate so fast that my face was plastered against it. That was how I had found out that the electrocution sign on the gate was bogus.

I speed-walked out of those gates and down the winding road in the hot July sun, and it was the best feeling in the world. My family were on their way to pick me up, but I was released before they got there. I was *not* going to wait inside for them to get there! I gave the "injustice" system twenty-eight long months of my life, and they were not about to get another second of my time, so I did what I enjoy doing the most and walked. Yup, I had gotten my walk on, and finally stopped at a bus shelter. Someone there was kind of enough to let me borrow their cell phone to call my mother to tell her that I had been released early and that I was waiting at the bus shelter.

Shortly thereafter, my family arrived, and had my clothes in the car with them. I did not care about those clothes. I jumped in the van wearing the state-issued clothing: ugly brown khakis, t-shirt, and those awful sweet potatoes (shoes). During my ride home, I lowered the window and stuck my head out to let the not-so-fresh air blow on my face. Of course, we were getting close to Philadelphia by then, because the air quality had changed. First stop was Rita's Water Ice (yes, I had made a list of food, things, and places while I was incarcerated), and that was the best mango water ice that I had ever had, and the worst brain freeze ever after I had devoured it. Second stop was home.

The rest of my family, friends, and neighbors were there, and greeted me with love and open arms. I was so happy to see them. After giving out plenty of hugs and kisses, a sister was ready to peel out of those state browns and jump in a hot bubble bath, which my mother or sister had prepared for me. Of course, that was the best bubble bath I'd had in a while. Once I was done, I took those dreadful state browns and trashed them in the outside trash can. Truth be told, I really wanted to burn them, but I went with the latter. My first meal home was a Philly cheesesteak from Max's—a chicken cheesesteak with mayo, light ketchup, fried onions, hot peppers, and provolone cheese. I could not wait to sink my teeth into it, and it was delicious.

The night began to fall, and I began doing my nightly routine: 150 crunches and stretching. I would do this routine every night, because it would help me get a good night's sleep. But my first night home was different. I was excited about sleeping in my own comfortable pillow-top bed, but sleep did not come easy. I guessed that I was anxious about being home. It was surreal. Eventually, though, I fell asleep. I was awakened in the morning by the sun beaming on my face, and I literally jumped out of bed and landed straight on my knees and started crying, praying, and saying thank you. I must have said thank you about a thousand times. I did not know what the day was going to bring, but what I did know was that I was free, and I was going to go for a walk.

My mother had bought me walking flip flops, and they were so comfortable. I mean, I would walk everywhere in them. When I say that I would walk I mean, I would walk. Also, I did not have a choice, because I was waiting for my driver's license to be reinstated. But I did not mind because I enjoy walking.

WALK OF SERENDIPITY

This one day, which was the second most memorable walk, I was walking down Germantown Avenue and noticed a hair salon that I had never seen before. I went into the salon and started speaking with one of the hairstylists, and after a few minutes, I decided to get my hair washed, blow dried, and curled.

While I was sitting under the dryer, I overheard a conversation between one of the hairstylists and a customer. The customer was telling the hairstylist that she was dating a guy and that the guy was a drug dealer. She also expressed how she was concerned about what came along with dating a guy that dealt drugs and how she felt uncomfortable. She also stated that she was a single mother of two young children and lived in low-income housing. But the money that he was giving her was helping her out as well, though he would sometimes bring drugs and guns into her home.

So, as I was sitting there taking in this conversation, I was like, *This cannot be true, someone is playing a trick on me.* What were the odds of me going on my daily walk and walking right into a salon and overhearing this conversation? It was meant to be! I believe things do not just happen. They are destined. Finally, I was up next to get my hair done, and when I sat down in the chair, the customer that was sharing her dilemma was still there. We greeted one another and she continued talking about her issues. After a while, I became engaged in the conversation and asked the young lady if she minded if I had shared my story with her.

I told her that I had been in a similar situation, dating a drug dealer. I shared how it had affected me and my family's lives. How I had missed my son's senior prom and high school graduation and how he was supposed to go to college and did not. How I had two family members that passed (one was my uncle, who I was close to), missed the birth of my first great niece, and how two of my childhood friends' grandmothers had passed while I was gone (those two women were part of my village while growing up). I told her how I lost my job and could not finish getting my degree (I had later received my degree), and the embarrassment of the police broadcasting my arrest on the news and in the newspaper. I explained to her how precious time is and that you cannot get it back, and most importantly, that her children should not be exposed to that type of lifestyle. That your home is their safe place, and that no one should be allowed to disrupt that, especially not a drug dealer that she didn't feel comfortable being with in the first place. If she felt that way, he did not need to be there. I told her to trust her gut, it would never fail her. I had also told her, "That man does not care about you or your children, because if he did, he would not subject you to that lifestyle." I told her that if she wasn't going to get rid of him for herself, she needed to do it for her children.

I know sometimes us women think that we are in love and that he can be the man of our dreams, but that is not always true. We can get blinded by the things that they do for us or give us, such as giving us material things, or just feelings of being loved. I also shared with her that some guys prey on young women like her—single moms struggling to raise their children on their own. They come along offering to help by buying material things and giving money. I got it. Yes, it may relieve some of the financial burden, but in the long run, it was not worth your life, freedom, and time. Meanwhile, he had a plan, to store his drugs and guns at her home, a place to rest his head, and only God knew what else. He was not worth it! A real man would not put you in a situation like that.

As I was telling them my story, the salon got so quiet that you have could hear a pin drop and the facial expressions were priceless. There were so many emotions up in there. One lady stated, "Omg, you do not look like the type!"

I asked her "What is the type?"

She said, "You know, the type to go to jail."

I said, "Well, I did not plan to go there, and I guess I am not the type, because that was my first and last time and I will never, ever walk through those gates again."

By the end of the story, the young lady was in tears and said she was going to go home and kick him out of her house.

A few months later, as I was driving by the salon, I pulled over and went in to ask the stylist about the young lady with the drug-dealing boyfriend.

She said, "Oh she went home that same day and kicked him out, and she is doing good."

I was so happy to hear the good news. I was touched that she had the courage to end the relationship, and extremely glad that my story had made such an impact that it encouraged her to take control of her life and get rid of that man, who did not mean her and her children any good.

I am a person who normally does not share my business with people who are not in my trusted circle, let alone a stranger. However, I was compelled to help this young lady before it was too late. I wanted to save her from experiencing the type of trauma that I had endured, or even worse. I was surprised at myself for having the courage to share my story; the old me would have sat there, tuned them out, and minded my business. I did not know what came over me, because I used to be embarrassed and ashamed about what happened to me, and I did not like talking about it. I just wanted to put the past behind me and move forward, because being ripped away from my home and family was traumatizing. Later, though, I realized that sharing my story helped me in many ways. I felt empowered and like a weight was lifted from me. It was very therapeutic. I am who I am, and those experiences contributed to me being the woman I am today. I turned my trauma into triumphs, denials into acceptance, fears into being fearless, sadness to happiness, and shame into being shameless.

Overall, I hope that my story can save families and as many lives as possible. I believe that everyone in the salon took something away from my story that day, including myself, whether it was to be courageous, trust your intuition, do not judge a book by its cover, or most importantly, do not take life for granted, because it can be altered within the blink of an eye.

WALK OF REFLECTION

I am blessed and grateful to have a great support system. Not everyone has that. I witnessed that while being incarcerated; family, friends, boyfriends, girlfriends, fiancés, husbands, etc. started falling off. They stopped answering phone calls, then their phone numbers were disconnected, visits that had once been once a week became once a month, and then turned into no visits at all. I know both sides of the coin. It can become a burden on family members to send money and take the time out to come visit. They have their own responsibilities to take care of. My heart used to ache for some of the women who had not had a visit or had seen their family in years and decades. I witnessed how the visiting room would be full of visitors, and as time went on, they became less and less common. Not to mention some of the things that I saw while being in there: the unfair treatment of inmates, inmates scheming, scamming and stealing from each other, being locked down for twenty-three hours a day, showering when you could (only in some of the housing units), eating what they wanted to feed you even when it wasn't enough. You can imagine some of the things that I saw. Some women performed sexual acts just to get food and snacks, because they did not have anyone putting money on their books and the pay they received from working in the prison was not enough, as they were working for 19 to 25 cents an hour (institutional slavery).

Sometimes when I sit back and think about the past, I say to myself, "Wow! You made it, you have a purpose, and you were not built to break!" I had to encourage myself with positive affirmations every single day, several times a day, and it worked. Because in the beginning of my incarceration, I did not think I was going to make it. I had always known I was a strong person, but I did not think I was strong enough to get through that ordeal. I am a critical thinker, the type who always find a loophole in any situation, but this one threw me for a loop, literally. I was devastated, hurt, angry, depressed, oppressed, and sad. Thank goodness it did not break me. I made a promise to myself that I would never allow anyone or anything to take me back to that state of mind ever again. The emotional scars are still there, they are part of me, now. It is my truth, and it is okay. I have accepted that. I can now talk about my past without feeling shameful, and I will always remember the day when my life took a drastic turn.

BOOM! BOOM!

"What the hell?!" I asked as I was awakened out of my sleep. It sounded like an explosion. I rolled over and shook my ex-boyfriend to wake him up, so that he could go and check out where the noise was coming from.

As soon as I rolled back over, a barrel of a shotgun was pointed at me.

It all happened so fast, and I had immediately froze. Three or four men dressed in black rushed into my bedroom and had their guns pointed at my ex-boyfriend. I felt this weird trembling, and when I looked over to my right, it was my ex-boyfriend shaking and trembling and begging them not to shoot him.

"Oh my God, What the hell is going on?! Please let me put some clothes on!" I yelled. The only thing I could think about was my teenage son. Still laying in my bed with my hands in the air, I just kept saying, "Please my son, my son!"

Then one of the men said to my ex-boyfriend, "You better keep your fat ass still before I shoot you!"

My ex-boyfriend continued to plead with them to not shoot him. He was shaking and moving so uncontrollably that I yelled out, "Stop moving before they shoot you!" And I was still in the bed with no clothes on and my hands in the air. Then finally a woman entered my bedroom and introduced herself.

"Where are your clothes?" she asked.

I had pointed toward the closet, which she opened. She began taking out clothes to give to me while the men then escorted my ex-boyfriend out of the room. Once they were gone, she began to help me put on my clothes. Once I had on my clothes, I asked, "Can you show me the warrant for his arrest? And could you speed it up, because I have to go to training for my job, and I cannot be late."

She said yes and reached into her back pocket, pulled out the paperwork, and stated, "I have two: One for him, and one for you."

Thursday, March 7, 2008 was one of the worst days of my life, *and* it was when it all began.

ACKNOWLEDGMENTS

thank you for allowing me to share part of my testimony. It was not an easy decision for me to make. I want to thank all of my family and friends who supported me through everything that I endured.

A special thanks to you, Delvia Y. Berrian, for considering me for this amazing project. You made this happen, and I am forever grateful!

Jéneen Barlow, thank you for making this process smooth and easy. I admire your dedication and professionalism. I look forward to working with you on my book.

Finally, to you who have read my story, I hope that I inspired you and touched your soul in the same way that sharing with you has touched mine.

You can read more about my story very soon.

Much love,

Tawanda

ABOUT THE AUTHOR

Tawanda Brookins is a native of Philadelphia, born and raised. She has one son, who she loves dearly and three grandchildren who she adores. She is a jack of all trades. Tawanda enjoys walking, cooking, decorating, traveling, shopping, and spending time making memories with her family and framily (friends that became family). In her free time, you will find her binge watching her favorite shows or movies, while sipping on a glass wine or one of her signature cocktails.

MESSAGE OF HOPE

RELENTLESS PURSUIT
LATRICE LE-ANN BOOKER

Therefore, since we have been justified by faith, we have peace with God through our Lord Jesus Christ. Through him we have also obtained access by faith into this grace in which we stand, and we rejoice in hope of the glory of God. Not only that, but we rejoice in our sufferings, knowing that suffering produces endurance, and endurance produces character, and character produces hope, and hope does not put us to shame, because God's love has been poured into our hearts through the Holy Spirit who has been given to us.
— Romans 5:1-5 ESV

Imagine getting in your car to drive to your destination without complications, error, or any accidental delays. You realize when you park your car, turn it off, and begin to step out that it was operated without you. There was no steering wheel that allowed you to direct the car to travel. The moment this revelation hits you, you identify with the overwhelming amount of peace and trust that lingered upon you. No worry, no wonder, no searching of how this could be possible... but only that there was a rest in trusting who made it possible. That being God Himself.

Let me share with you three stories that signify this level of trust that would produce a hope that would go beyond what was understood. Stories that we can all in some way identify with. To the point of that pivotal moment, just like in that dream. When you realize you've reached your destination without your hands on the wheel. This, my friend, should allow you to release your control of the direction of your life and rest in the understanding of the direction.

Let's travel down a path of discovering hope, when you are able to trust God through it all. Our journey begins in the book of 1 Kings, Chapter 17, beginning at Verse 2. We find the prophet Elijah resting at a brook after following God's instructions carefully. "And the word of the Lord came to him: 'Depart from here and turn eastward and hide yourself by the brook Cherith, which is east of the Jordan. You shall drink from the brook, and I have commanded the ravens to feed you there.' So he went and did according to the word of the Lord. He went and lived by the brook Cherith that is east of the Jordan."

Elijah was directed to the brook because, after declaring to king A'hab that a drought was to come, God commanded that he go and hide at the brook. Although Elijah did not have any more than that direction, he was alerted in the instructions that provisions would be provided. While he traveled, not only were provisions to be made, but God assured the prophet that it would come to be by the use of the brook and ravens. "'You shall drink from the brook, and I have commanded the ravens to feed you there.'" The passage shares that Elijah did according to the word of the Lord. He allowed God to direct the way.

We have all been in a place where we received instruction and moved forward with all diligence, trusting and holding on to God's assurance that we would be covered and provided for. But can you still move forward when the provision ceases?! 1 Kings 17:7 stated the "brook dried up," with this being the real question of whether you are able to remain faithful with keeping your hands off the wheel and continue to trust God through it all. Or will your reality become that you are tempted to take matters into your own hands and attempt to figure it out through your own understanding? If you and I are honest, we may try to begin to work it out for ourselves, trying to make sense of why our provision has come to end and beginning to find other means to replace what has stopped. Seeing its outcome through a half-focused perspective, a perspective that prevents us from keeping sight of God in the midst of our circumstances. Neglecting to maintain focus in the initial directions given and the promise He spoke.

When God gave the instructions, He also provided the provision, as well as asking us to move forward with the instructions. Elijah chose to keep his hands off the wheel and continued to trust God. When the prophet made the choice to keep trusting, God continued to bring forth greater provision, and with that provision, the prophet postured a continual trust unto God, allowing Him to direct his way. Elijah teaches us through his experience that when you take hold of the instructions without delay, provision and promise is given. We must develop a stronger hope through learning just how to trust the unknown that's before us.

This leads us to our next discovery of hope. Joseph's life was a journey of twists and turns, which would propel him toward the dream God had declared unto him. Joseph was met with many obstacles at the tender age of seventeen. He was loved by his father a bit more than his siblings, which caused great envy amongst them. They held onto this contempt, despising their brother in their hearts. Joseph had dreams that revealed that he would reach a place of leadership and change. We find the depth of God's revelation of his dreams in Genesis:

> His brothers said to him, "Are you indeed to reign over us? Or are you indeed to rule over us?" So they hated him even more for his dreams and for his words. Then he dreamed another dream and told it to his brothers and said, "Behold, I have dreamed another dream. Behold, the sun, the moon, and eleven stars were bowing down to me." But when he told it to his father and to his brothers, his father rebuked him and said to him, "What is this dream that you have dreamed? Shall I and your mother and your brothers indeed come to bow ourselves to the ground before you?" And his brothers were jealous of him, but his father kept the saying in mind.
>
> — Genesis 37: 8-11 ESV.

Within his dreams, God's plans were being carefully shared with this young lad. He would begin to see a glimpse into his journey, being privy to the latter result of that journey ahead. God not only brought attention to Joseph about what to anticipate, but was also making it known to his family that God's favor would be with Joseph. This caused his brothers to grow more bitter, but his father pondered it. The new revelation catapulted Joseph's life, making a change quickly and drastically, as his brothers conspired against him with efforts to harm him. But God used them to bring Joseph great favor. They lured him into the wilderness with the intent to kill him and leave him in a pit. They later made a choice to not harm him, but still trapped him in a pit alone. After more deliberation, they decided to stage his murder to cover their tracks and then sell him to the Midianities. His brothers hated him so much that they felt they were better off without him. Although this is only half of the twist and turns that Joseph encountered, the passage never shows Joseph doing anything other than maintaining integrity and uprightness. His journey reflects consistency and steadfastness.

Joseph went on to encounter many trying times. He faced being sold a second time to Potiphar, as he was subjected to more enslavement. Despite it all, God's favor rested on him. Under the possession of Potiphar, Joseph was met with even greater opposition. Faced with the attempt of being seduced and false allegations being presented against him by Potiphar's wife, Joseph could yet again not catch a break. But Joseph never tried to force his own control within the situation. He rested in the vision and favor of God alone. He remained in a posture of honor and integrity, despite having his life disrupted, uprooted, and stripped away. How many of us can say that when life traumas and changes hit, we can rest, knowing God has it all figured out? As much as I desire to always maintain that level of calmness, I can't say that I am capable of always modeling this characteristic.

Joseph, however, models something we can all aspire to do with how he managed life's ups and downs. He would eventually reach the palace, after being falsely accused. During his trying moments, while in jail, he met a man that would catapult him forward into a shift. A shift that would represent a revelation that Joseph had been shown some time earlier. Although it did not happen speedily, it still represented another level of hope and a deeper trust. It would all start with another dream. It was there that Joseph would be able to share his gift of interpretation of dreams. Joseph's request to the man after the interpretation was simple, but would be pivotal: to remember him when he reached Pharaoh. Pivotal because Pharaoh reigned over all the land. Having his natural favor could bring a release out of enslavement.

Although the remembrance was delayed, Joseph was eventually sought when Pharaoh himself requested an interpretation of his dream. Such a task would release Joseph to God's awaited promise that had been shared in his dreams many years earlier. Joseph would be blessed by Pharaoh to receive his ring and reign over all of Egypt. He gained great honor through his faithfulness. This task would be the opportunity for Joseph to reunite with his family. Through it all, Joseph trusted the path, thought he might not have anticipated or desired it. Nevertheless, he did not try to disrupt the ways in which he encountered life on his journey. He showed a posture of faith, maintaining a great hope that God's promises, which were shared in his initial dreams, would come to fruition. Through his many twists and turns, he built a strong trust, his faith was made greater, and his promise was received.

These two stories are just a few of the many examples we can use to gain wisdom and understanding. Joseph's journey teaches us that although what was promised may tarry, that hardship may hit, that your support may become distant, He assures us that His presence and favor will continue.

These stories teach us how to effectively connect to God. They reflect a proper response of willingness to yield to God's plans, as these men eliminated their own plans for how their paths would be laid out. I, too, experienced twists and turns through many hills and valleys. Each rounding corner I encountered, every tumbling fall that led me toward the fighting climbs back up the hill, was a story being born through me that would convey assurance and hope. Just like that dream, imagine being in that car and traveling through the pathway before you, convinced that you are in control. You have it all handled and worked out. You display what you believe is confidence, knowing that the journey is being carefully pursued. Confident that you will arrive at the destination unscathed. Mapping out the route of travel in what you characterize as your own understanding, with the result that you will arrive there successfully. But just like in that dream, you reach that place and realize that you were never in charge of steering the wheel.

The prophet Elijah and Joseph both recognized this when they reached the greater purpose through their experiences, however I myself would also come to learn it through peaks and valleys. It was a pivotal moment in my life and a transformation that would really bring me to my knees. I realized I was never controlling the wheel. I simply came to understand that I rested in the hands of the One that was.

This shift would begin for me with a question asked of me while I was praying. The question God would ask of me was one He knew the answer to, though He desired that I consider the response. It was a question that would challenge me to examine just how I laid my life out before Him. To shake up how I pursued Him, and take me deeper, beyond the accustomed safe places of the surface when it came to our relationship. God simply asked me, "Latrice, do you not trust Me, I will restore?"

The moment this question was spoken, it touched my soul and brought me to attention. It was a question that I could answer with a hesitant yes. I can admit that I was not able to be definitive and precise with my response, if I'm honest. Not that I didn't have trust in God. It was because I knew that I trusted Him with what I wanted to let go of. I still wanted to be the gatekeeper of a lot of things in my life. I struggled with admitting that and being accountable to it, and God knew this. He wanted me to recognize this. He needed me to own it, so it could change. He needed this behavior to cease and be dismantled within me. It was subtle habits that would affect how my behavior was modeled before Him. Not only was God calling my attention to His question, which required a response; He also followed it up with a promise. He simply showed me what I wasn't doing, and the reason for the reluctance. My lack of trust in areas uncovered the fact that I desired security and knowing that I could let go without any doubt. If I'm honest, I let go mostly, but quietly kept my hand on things a bit, ready to take back control when things looked like they were going array. It became so second-nature that I never even realized it was how I approached God within our relationship. I was not allowing Him the freedom to move as He pleased. I was trying to keep Him in a box, but that was the pride and foolish thinking we tend to have. God can never be put within a confined space—not even the confinement of our thoughts. He has even made it clear to us, as He declares in His word that His thoughts are not our thoughts, neither are our ways His ways. It's a constant battle to understand this. It was not until this question was asked that I began to deal with the blatant denial. When God asks you a question, believe He already knows the answer. The question is for you to become accountable to Him and yourself and acknowledge what is being asked of you. I was so stuck that I would have never been able to realize that at that moment, I would be presented with a strenuous study lesson.

Instantly, God began to teach me the depth of trusting Him, much like the passage in Proverbs 3 declares that we have to trust in the Lord with all our heart, and not lean on our own understanding.

But we are to acknowledge Him, and He will lay out our paths. I had to face my truth of hesitation and let Him lead the way. When the question was asked, it required me to be stretched, which meant that I would undergo being stripped. Stripped of what I believed to be secure to be certain to me through my understanding. Here I go yet again, trying to navigate through learning how to trust Him with my understanding being the end goal. With my reasoning, the way that steps are taken, and with my perspective being the desired resolved to the question. God would soon make clear to me that my hand was not on the wheel, but that He would be determining the road that was to be traveled.

When you are being prepared to be used by God to bring glory to His name and break barriers for others, you are going to experience a place of wilderness in your life. Much like Elijah and Joseph, I would be given a directive and a promise. With this, He meant for me to move forward. Moving forward and no longer clutching on to what was securing to me. It would begin with the shaking of relationships. Friendships being removed, recalibrated, and realigned. Family relationships being tested for durability. Experiencing trying workdays consistently, as the enemy sought to find his daily host that he could use to initiate his taunting.

When the lesson began, it refused to teach me lightly. When it hit, it all came at once. Navigating through so many areas of what felt like brokenness made me try to grab hold of what I could to maintain. To keep control. But the more I grasped for control, the more I kept realizing that I had none. I wasn't grasping that the lessons were meant to *break* my control. My way, my habit of needing to steer the wheel. The hit would start with the external that I kept so securely fastened to me. The thought of my outer world being shaken made me withdraw and retreat to a space that I could guard myself. Taking a hit to every relationship in your life brings questions about who really cares. It forces you to take inventory of what you really have security in. You think about your friends, family relationships, your career, your future. But when life hits hard, none of those things are guaranteed to remain consistent. The external things can't provide security, because if we are honest, they are also one life-changing moment away from experiencing a similar thing.

I would also come to understand this all the more through my own experiences. The more I recognized that what I relied on would no longer be willing to help me, the more it stung, and it stung hard. The sting brought about a daze that would cause me to forget how to dream. My hurt and loss dominated my expectations. I felt robbed of choice and opportunity. I was in a desolate place, and I could not bear to even try to make an effort to change it. I knew that at that moment, I needed help. I was going to have to push forward, through my fleeting feelings and to what was embedded inside of me. The Lord would remind me of His promise. He told me that He knew the plans that He had for me—plans to help me grow, not harm me, and plans that would bring hope and a future. This reminder gave me what I needed to anchor in and hold fast to. It was needed because I had not gone through the heart of the storm just yet.

As the lesson continued, I was met with even greater opposition. I had to face reality and navigate through rejection, embarrassment, shame, heartbreak, slander, affliction, being misunderstood, grief, unworthiness, defaced value, perplexity, bewilderment, and loss of relationships and bonds, as well as the realization that things weren't how they appeared to me previously. On top of this, I had to deal with being a mother of two children that depended on me to show up and be present. As I dealt with the many emotions that rose inside, on the outside, I did my best to keep it together. I struggled to care for my children, as my finances were extremely shaken. I simply had nothing. I survived in this season with the blessing of being able to overdraft my account just to keep up with payments. Knowing that it only caused more strain, as it made more financial burdens.

During this period, we stayed with relatives, which started well, but was not a burden they could commit to for the long-term. Their help eventually reached its end. With this, my children and I transitioned to an even smaller space—a tension-filled environment, that was welcomed only partially. We always felt like we were in the way and a burden on those that extended what help they could. This caused even more emotional hardship and strain. Experiencing this period of homelessness, we traveled from relative to relative, staying as long as the grace remained. Grateful to God that my children and I did not have to face the life of shelters, or even worse, of living outside like so many. But the contemplation and worry would soon come to be. A thought that I would have to closely consider. Yet again, the transition of needing to relocate knocked at the door, and this time, there was no place to go. I was given the harsh reality that my children and I would need to pack up and move no matter whether we had a residence available. The words rang loud in my head after they were spoken. Hurt filled my heart. I was broken. How much more could I endure? Can you imagine the terror as a woman, a mother, having to prepare your children to accept the fact that being homeless might be an immediate truth? The thought that we may have to relocate to a shelter, or even worse, our car, was terrifying. To this day, I can still feel the intensity of the emotion that came over me in that season. Having to contemplate where we would maintain daily hygienic practices, and safe areas to idle so we can rest at the end of the day. It was a period in my life when

I wondered just how I'd arrived at that point. I never could have imagined that would be my reality, but sadly, it was.

The anguish I was in continued to intensify. I was battling anxiety and depression simultaneously, as I was fighting despair while being attacked by constant thoughts racing within. I realize even more that I was not in control. I could not figure this out on my own. It was going to take me continuing to seek God and find my safe space in Him. He made it clear to me that He was near, although I had great adversity. While everything around me seemed to be crumbling, God began to start magnifying those behavioral traits, making clear to me what was blocking me from trusting Him. Showing me how pride quietly crept in and was the culprit for my lack of trust. Not being willing and able to admit I needed help and accept it. Challenging me to deal with where this first took root. A root I didn't realize would be a survival trait for having to navigate life without a lot of help.

How I interacted with others affected how I treated God. I did not allow the opportunity for Him to shower me with His abundance. He began to uncover so many faulty things that were quietly embedded in some of my habits. Lingering of unforgiveness, fear, rejection, inadequacy, insecurity, and lack of self-worth. I was on one wild ride, and this ride made me fasten my seatbelt and just stay still. I stayed on my knees, laying on my face before the Lord, and sought to be quiet and rest in His presence. The more I went through, the more I learned to forget about trying to control it all and bring my own reasoning to everything I endured. His presence became even more heightened. He would position people near me that were not familiar, but it was clear that they were ordained to walk alongside me. Opportunities came to be, just like with Abraham and the ram in the bush. God would bring all that I needed. During my trying moments and the fear of being without a home, I was challenged to either trust or worry. I had no way of my own to provide the needs for shelter; no financial outlet that could rent anything. My means were in the red, and I had nothing.

I could either declare defeat... or take a leap of faith and trust God.

I chose the latter. I chose to do what was beginning to grow within me since being on this journey, which was praying without ceasing. Worshiping through my pain, trusting that there was a greater purpose in my press. I had nothing other than this—no potential place, no money to get the place, no idea of how the plan was going to come together. I simply trusted God. I trusted and believed that He would provide. I was certain of it. The time grew closer and closer to the day when I would be told that we must leave with no hesitation. Literally two weeks before the date, as I searched Craigslist, a site that was truly out of the norm for me to look for living spaces, I came across an apartment that I felt would be in my budget. I felt good about the prospect of it in my spirit. It was a peace that came over me. I went and looked at it, and knew that was my place. In the midst of that, I unexpectedly received a school refund that would be the very amount that I needed to make the move.

Everything was coming together.

I kept trusting and believing in faith that change was underway. A few days later, I got the response. I was not approved for the apartment. Now, just a week away from needing to move, I still had no place to go, but I kept saying, "God, I trust you. It's going to work out." The owner did something that was not typical for him: asked me the background to my troubled credit history. Just wanting to hear my story, to understand. I shared my truth with him, vulnerable and stripped of my pride. I was open and vulnerable, able to finally rest and know that I was secure. That night, the owner listened to me and asked if he could share my name with any others that could be of help. I graciously accepted, and was truly grateful. I knew that God was using him to be a vessel on my behalf. I knew in my gut that God still had it worked out, and believed that that was my home. The owner unexpectedly called me a few days later to tell me that he was willing to look beyond my application challenges to provide housing to me and my children. That if I was still interested, he would like to move forward, and do so quickly.

The deadline was met and we were finally blessed, after many trying years, with a place to call home. The owner would go on to be even more amazing throughout the years. He was an example of God choosing to send His help through another person, allowing me to receive from an unfamiliar, unexpected vessel. There were others that He would send my way. To stand with me, hold me up, and pray me through. God began to form a core of individuals as He started to reconstruct my outer parameter. While the outer was becoming durable, He also continued to fortify the inner places of me. I began to find my voice in prayer. I understood more and more about my strength and releasing to the help of the Holy Spirit. Taking the pressures off of me and resting under His wings.

Not many even knew all that I went through, because I kept bearing the pressure that was there and simply trusting God through it. The harsher the journey became, the more I spent my nights and days praying and seeking the presence of God. I literally spent my nights on the floor, crying and wailing in prayer. It was the only place I felt safe to let go. My tears carried so many prayers that it unlocked my place of worship before the Lord. It was there that I started to realize that God was doing something new that would transform me for good. I was given a song that I would start humming within the depths of my soul. I carried the words of Psalm 40 very near. A promise that rang louder than any words anyone ever spoke to me. For I kept affirming,

I waited patiently for the Lord; he inclined to me and heard my cry. He drew me up from the pit of destruction, out of the miry bog, and set my feet upon a rock, making my steps secure. He put a new song in my mouth, a song of praise to our God. Many will see and fear, and put their trust in the Lord. Blessed is the man who makes the Lord his trust, who does not turn to the proud, to those who go astray after a lie! You have multiplied, O Lord my God, your wondrous deeds and your thoughts toward us; none can compare with you! I will proclaim and tell of them, yet they are more than can be told.

The daily affirmation of this promise brought life to my bones and showed me strength in the Lord. It pressed me to seek purpose and meaning, and opened my heart to dream again. Hope was restored, desire was growing. I found reason and meaning in life that could not be tampered with. I had a song of worship that I found in what I thought to be hopeless, but it was being given. The question that was asked would be my challenge. To live its lesson so that I would never hesitate with the question or the response. The many twists and turns helped me learn that I never had control of the wheel, and it was for my benefit. I would learn so much through my loss.

As I reflect and write about all I've learned and what was lost through this journey, I hear the sweet whisper of the Lord gently speaking over me. "My worship awaited you!" This astounding truth was gently nudged into my spirit; words whose purpose was not to be accompanied by fireworks or any big burst of revelation. Rather, the words were meant to incite my soul within. Through a still small voice came great revelation, just like powerful, rushing ocean waters that meet the sands of the beach. The gentle whisper met my inward parts, causing my soul to leap. Oftentimes, when a song is sung and that melody is carried by a songstress in an amazing way, it causes the response of individuals receiving chills upon the surface of their skin. In much the same way, I felt the effects of this lingering upon my heart.

To receive such a quiet, profound embrace and reinforcement places you in an awe-inspiring place. As I rested in that revelation, I couldn't help but linger with the thought that yes, God wanted my undivided attention. He wanted me to fully commit and connect to Him. The beauty found in this was Him wanting me to simply receive Him. God's desire was that I would long for Him alone. That nothing more could grasp or keep my attention. That I was really wanting to forsake it all to lay in His presence. These nights spent laid out before the Lord were intentional. It was our appointment time. Carved out to release and reach for God alone. It was a sacred place to lay before the Lord and latch onto Him even the more. He was ready for me to lay down and rest. The Lord was inviting me to lay low to unleash my longing for Him. Through this press, I learned to worship all the more.

My press was similar to the sentiments from David's heart in Psalm 40. Through His time of pressing into the presence of God, in the midst of his adversity, a song was crafted into the depths of his soul. He cried out and God cultivated His words through him. He opened his heart to render reverence and honor in the midst of his pain. My worship was learned through the wilderness; although I was faced with adversity, it released an unrelenting audacity within me. Every challenge was given to me so that I would charge forward boldly, trusting Him. Building my faith and forsaking my fears. Yes, I was met with weakened relationships, shaken foundations, and the threat of shelter being stripped away. I chose to trust all the more. All of these external factors didn't even speak to the heart surgery God was working inside of this wretched vessel of mine. And yet, I chose to grasp of what was spoken to me at the beginning. The question held a directive and a promise. The question was stated so plainly: "Latrice, do you not trust Me? I will restore." It was a call to respond. He wasn't asking because He was unclear. He asked because He wanted *me* to get clear. To ready myself with learning just how to do so. And once I learned a lesson and became clear on it, I would never forget.

Through the wilderness as worship would find my lips, I did not yet fully see the fruition of my cries. My lips would release songs in the midst of my heart-wrenching pain. Even while I waited to see the release of my prayers, I cried out with adoration. I gave the Lord my best when I faced being battered by the battle I was in. These were nights that I spent before Him, wailing. I consciously inclined my ear, knowing that He would restore. The more I rested, the stronger my trust grew. Through the meekness of my heart, it built the power of His might within. When I had only the space of a room, the Lord allowed me to fill every ounce of it with sounds of worship. Allowing me to release my prayers for mercy, seeking to draw closer to Him and learn the undeniable parts of His character I never came to truly know.

During my wailing, I lingered all the more in the Lord's presence. This place of intimacy allowed me to learn my identity. Identity that was understood when I embraced His. The Lord invited me into His embrace. My worship was personal! It was a release of my reverence unto Him, the adoration my soul released unto the Lord. I dove deep into my Savior's arms, and found myself pressing to lay before the Lord. It drew me to receive unrestricted, and in this place, I grew. I groaned for my Lord, and in return, He engraved His love into me all the more.

This place wasn't solely for me to release my worship or my wailing. It was also where I released my will and my way. The Lord welcomed me into His presence, to share the inscriptions of His love for me.

This is a place we can all obtain as we lay before the Lord. The journeys of each of these stories may resemble parts of your life. They may carry the manuscript to your story, a story that is being crafted and getting ready to be told. Each of these stories had their paths, and yet inspiration was able to be found. Elijah was sustained and provided for through a famine, proving that the provision of God's hand was upon him. Joseph was preserved and protected through countless moments of abandonment and being a prisoner, as he was provided an undeniable security from God. And my own testimony, finding assurance and certainty through a trying fire of adversity, is the culmination. My life was tried, producing triumph in it. Job shares it so eloquently in Chapter 24: "But he knows the way that I take; when he has tried me, I shall come out as gold."

Through the trials, trust was birthed. What was expected of me to be made clear came to be. Through my pain, I was released to His presence on purpose. Just like these journeys, you, too, can be met with more. It was as if He needed to rip it all away so He would be the only thing left for me to wrap myself in. Allowing yourself to let go of the wheel and let God direct you is a step toward showing that He matters. Loosen the grip on your life, reveal that you never held tightly to it, anyhow. There was only a constant grappling to continue to catch before you crash. But the secret is calling out for the mercy of God, which carries over into our lives the blessing of His grace. Once we relinquish our hands, our ways, our will, we can wholeheartedly embrace His, alone. Here, we find assurance that His thoughts are good toward us. Knowing this breaks us out of the ways of restrictive rest within His Will. This behavior is destructive, and delays our route of travel. Disrupting the ease of its journey that is harmful for the intended end. As the inherit children of the King, we each have been promised an abundant life in Christ Jesus, within the wait of the abundance. Just like in these three stories, abandoning your course of travel will result in great triumph.

ABOUT THE AUTHOR

Latrice Le-Ann Booker is a native of Philadelphia, Pennsylvania. She is the proud mother of two; a son, Jabri Amir, and a daughter, Abria Noel. She has worked in the medical field for the past 15 years as a medical assistant, as well as, a clinical coordinator. Latrice received her Bachelor's in Psychology with a focus in counseling and therapy, from the University of Valley Forge. Latrice has since begun furthering her studies to grow deeper in her love for God's Word, at Dallas Theological Seminary, where she is currently pursuing her Master of Theology.

Latrice is a faithful member of Greater Exodus Baptist Church, under the leadership of Reverend, Dr. Herbert H. Lusk II. Currently she serves on the youth leadership team, as the Assistant Director of the Women's Ministry, and as the Head of Member Care.

Latrice has a great love for writing and empowering others through encouragement and love. She is the recently published author of the *Crown Your Vision with Purpose Planner*, which is a devotional planner created to propel women closer to their destiny and purpose. The planner is designed to equip women not only to set goals, but to capture the mind of Christ while doing so.

She truly sets out each day to share the beauty of Christ that resides within her heart. Although Latrice has accomplished a lot, there is still so much more that is to come.

Latrice's truest joy is to simply be a servant of Christ and a vessel of honor for His divine mission!

"But I do not account my life of any value nor as precious to myself, if only I may finish my course and the ministry that I received from the Lord Jesus, to testify to the gospel of the grace of God"

— Acts 20:24 ESV

MESSAGE OF HOPE 3

MESSAGE OF HOPE

THE DEEP END OF THE OCEAN
STACI LA`MARR MORGAN

*Being confident of this very thing, that he which hath begun a
good work in you will perform it until the day of Jesus Christ.*
                                              — Philippians 1:6

As a young child, I always loved the beach. My family spent summers in Martha's Vineyard. I remember playing by the edge of the ocean while my dad and grandfather fished. The rule was always to stay close to the beach, because if I went too far into the water, I could get pulled in and possibly under the water and drown. As I got a little older, my love for the beach continued to increase. I had taken swimming lessons when I attended summer camp, and yet my mother still had that golden rule not to go too far into the ocean, for fear that I could go under the water and not survive. The older I got, the more curious I became about going farther into the ocean. I thought to myself, I could swim, so what would be the harm in going farther out?

I recall that as I continued increasing my desire to be in water, there was a person who had the responsibility to monitor swimmers who were in large bodies of water such as a pool, lake, or

43

ocean. They sat up high on these tall chairs so they could see everyone in the water and ensure that everyone was being safe and following the rules for the area they were charged to watch. They were equipped with a whistle and a life preserver, which was used to keep someone afloat in the water in the event that they needed to execute a rescue. Every now and then, I would hear the whistle being blown by the lifeguard, and when you heard that sound, it signified that a swimmer was at risk for drowning. After the guard got the attention of the swimmer (s), they would direct them to a safe area.

I am a parallel thinker, so I began to think about how wise the concept of a lifeguard was. Having someone to watch and let you know when you are drifting too far into deep water caused me to think about how God was that lifeguard for me during a very dark period in my life. If you are fortunate, you are out in the far end of the ocean with someone else. But I got to thinking, what if no one was with you way out in the ocean? What if the lifeguard was blowing the whistle and you didn't hear it? What if the lifeguard could not reach you? What would you use to stay afloat until someone could rescue you?

Ironically, as I was processing this water experience, I was surfing TV stations, looking for something worthwhile to watch. I landed on watching *Titanic*. This well-known movie, based on a true story about a sinking ship, pushed my mind into deeper thoughts. The scene was the final moments of the movie, where Jack and Rose had jumped into the cold, deep Atlantic Ocean after the ship was fully submerged into the water. It was dark, freezing temperatures, debris was all around them, and other people were out in the deep end of the ocean. Some were struggling to stay afloat, to stay alive without a life preserver, without a lifeguard, and without the sound of a whistle to alert them that danger was close. To a degree, Jack could have been Rose's lifeguard. He allowed her to lay on the door from the ship, which kept her afloat. During a rescue, the lifeguard remains in the water while the person being saved uses the life preserver to remain above the water. When it looked like Rose was giving up, when it looked like she was giving in, he started to speak life into her. The evidence all around them looked dark and hopeless, but he made her promise to hold on and never let go.

What I found to be profound was that Jack and Rose jumped into the water in order to save themselves. There was no one saying, "Don't go too far into the ocean, because you might drown." They took a chance that it was better to jump in than to sink in. One would think that they had some preconceived notions about this decision. You might think that they thought they would have some level of control if the choice to jump in was theirs.

I realized that my life took a similar journey. Not on a ship that was never built to sink, but on a cruise voyage in my life, where everything was smooth sailing on a course called, "Destination: happy place." My career was going well. My daughter was growing into a positive young lady. My mom was living with us and we hadn't killed each other. I had rededicated my life back to Christ, I had yielded a "yes" to God, and I was anticipating turning forty years old on February 14, 2008. Then my mom got sick the day before the observed day set aside to honor the life of M. L. King, Jr. She was rushed to the hospital that day, and we learned that she had an enormous lump in her breast. The alarms went off in my head. What was this doctor talking about? I even had the nerve to get spicy with him when he was talking to me. They ran a series of tests in order to determine what would happen next. Like when the panic began on *Titanic*, I began having thoughts racing around in my head like the people were racing around on the ship. I wanted answers, but I had to wait for the results to come back.

My birthday finally arrived, and my mom had a doctor's appointment on that day. We went for her appointment, and as we waited for the doctor to come in to see us, anxiety was building. I couldn't find the courage or the strength like Jack displayed during that waiting period. Finally, in comes the doctor. Test results were reviewed, it was like listening to the band on the ship playing their final set before the bow plunged into the water. The results were quickly heading for the iceberg, and in the next moment, we heard "You have Stage 4 cancer."

Talk about crashing into an iceberg. My entire life shattered into pieces, just like the ship. I felt like the Titanic, with pieces of my heart breaking and flying all over the place. Landing in almost every part of the ocean. Like Rose, my life looked dismal. I could not imagine how my heart would go on without the woman who gave me life. Who nurtured me. Who taught me everything that I knew about being a strong, independent woman and mother. My mom and Jack held on to their hope and breathed it into me and Rose. They both released their lives and passed. Rose drifted in the ocean on a piece of debris that kept her afloat. That debris was her life preserver.

I, too, found myself drifting into the deepest end of the ocean in my life. No lifeguard to warn me that I was drifting into danger emotionally, spiritually, and mentally. For many days, weeks, months, and even years, I was cold and it was dark in my life even when it was daylight. There was mental debris all around me. There were fragments of my heart everywhere. There was spiritual death encamping around me. At many points in my life, I thought I was going to lose my mind. Jack made Rose promise not to let go, but I unlike Rose, I let go. Not of my mother's hands, but of God's hands.

Because I let go of His unchanging hands, I drifted further and further out into the deep end of the ocean. I separated myself from Him. I was so angry with God. I could not process how I could pray and fast for her healing, and yet He took my mom. I served in His ministries, I studied His word, I prayed, I loved people that I truly didn't want to love, and yet in three short months, my mom was gone. I found myself drifting further and further out into the ocean. So far out that if I were at the beach and there was a lifeguard on duty, he would have blown his whistle to signal to me that I was out too far. Where was my lifeguard? Why didn't I hear the signal to let me know that I was out too far?

My drifting continued for years. My anger continued for years. The distance between me and God went on for years. I was a complete and total mess. That was why I couldn't hear the whistle from God. And if I was not already out in the deepest end of the ocean, in 2011 still angry, still drifting, now I lost my last living parent. My father had now passed away. I thought, *This will truly be my Jack moment. I am just going to let go and drown in the sea.* Most people would have stayed angry and broken, subsequently leaving the church. Continuing to separate farther and farther from God. Not me. I stayed angry and distraught but remained in the church. If you remember in the movie, Jack was a stowaway and Rose was from a prominent family. Jack received a nice tuxedo to wear to dinner so that he could fit in with the elite. I was Jack, masking who I was underneath the nice-looking attire on the outside called Deaconess Staci. My church facade masked my broken heart. I had a peaceless mind and there was very little joy to be found in my life. My soul was wrought with grief, and I had a mind that was far from being on Jesus.

Fast forward, and now I have elevated in ministry leadership to Evangelist Staci and like Jack, I became good at looking like someone else. I became good at looking like a believer, but in reality, I was truly a sinner that had fallen down. I had fallen so far that it didn't look like I could get back up. Why was I a sinner? I'm glad you asked. I was lying about my emotional, mental, and spiritual state. The Bible tells us in Proverbs 12:22, "The Lord detests lying lips." Every time someone asked me how I was doing, how I was holding up since the loss of my mom and dad, I said, "I'm good. I'm working through it." Lie after lie. The drifting continued, and I was so far out in the deep end of the ocean that it started to get quiet. Just like it did in the movie. You could at one time hear the people screaming, moaning, crying out for help. After a period of time, it became quiet. All that could be heard was the waves from the wind blowing against the water. 1 Kings 19:12 talks about "After the earthquake there was a fire and after the fire there was a still small voice." I could not hear a voice, still or otherwise, because I was still angry with God.

In a matter of three years, my life had been turned upside down, just like the lives of those that embarked on a luxury ship sailing for their Destination Happy Place. A crash into an iceberg and their lives would never be the same. The loss of two parents in a three-year time span and my life has never been the same. The aftermath of my emotional, spiritual, and mental crash into that iceberg of unresolved grief and loss took me deeper and deeper and deeper into the ocean. The blessing was that I could swim, but I was definitely treading water to stay afloat. Dishonesty about my grief and loss began to be anchors in my life. It was there, the weight was heavy. And I just kept treading in the water.

Now I was so deep in the ocean that by clinical standards, I became functionally depressed. I couldn't even feel that I was bobbing up and down in the ocean. Still maintaining my facade that I got it all together. Still being dishonest when people asked me how I was doing. Poor decision after poor decision. Inviting innocent people to go along on the journey into the deep end of the ocean with me. I couldn't help them, and I couldn't help myself. So deep in the ocean that I didn't realize that the role model I desired to be for my daughter, I was missing the mark big time. Everything I didn't want to teach her, I ended up doing. Now I was out in the deep end of the ocean and I brought the most precious jewel God trusted me with along on the journey with me. Who compromises their child's emotional, spiritual, and mental destiny? How did I get here? Me, the super social worker who could assess everyone else's life, and give them a plan to follow, but missed the whole boat for her own life. No pun intended.

I hurt someone on this cruise ship of destruction because I didn't practice safety in the water like I had been taught when I was learning how to swim. I remembered my instructor telling me, "The water can be your friend or your enemy." You get to decide which one it will be. I remember lying in bed one morning and talking to God. I was so heavy and joyless. Tears began to stream down my face. I looked up and said, "God, this can't be the life you have for me." That day, at that moment, I heard God say, "It's not the life I have for you." **I looked up.** Psalm 121:1 reminded me, "I will lift up mine eyes until the hills, from whence cometh my help." Finally, I heard the whistle. I heard God's voice. Rose was laying on the debris looking up to the heavens, and then she heard a still voice say, "Hello, is anybody out there?" She got her help. She got her strength. Rose whispered to Jack and said, "I won't let go. I will never let go." As she gently released his hands, he slid into the water. She treaded through the water over to a body that had a whistle and blew it. Remember, I shared that the lifeguard was equipped with a whistle that could be used to signal swimmers in order to direct or guide them to safety. For Rose, when she blew the whistle, it guided the boat toward her. They would then rescue her from the deep waters and take her to safety.

For me, when I said, "God this can't be the life you had planned for me," and He responded that it wasn't, that was when I heard the whistle. It was God's still small voice that guided me out of the deepest end of the ocean and back into the safety of His loving and forgiving arms.

Have you ever felt like *you* are or were too broken, flawed, angry, bitter, or weak to be used by God? Are you serving in ministry or did you used to serve in ministry, but because of your wrinkles, your spots, your blemishes, you feel like you are too much of a mess, or you decided that because of your not-so-perfect state, you had to leave the ministry or even your church?

I have some great news for you! Throughout scripture, you will find that God used broken, angry, spotted, blemished, wrinkled, and any other bad or negative characteristic you can think of to achieve His divine glory and I pray that my story gives you assurance why this is so even today.

I invite you to travel back in time with me. The Apostle Paul was one of the most influential Christian leaders of his time. He was a teacher and a writer and embraced his ordained assignment to spread the gospel, as well as to provide instructions on "how" to live as Christians. One may ask, "How could he write and give encouragement to others or teach anyone anything when he had made so many mistakes, which included murder?" From the outside eye, with all of those mistakes, he had to feel like he disappointed God.

I know after my deep end-of-the-ocean experience, I felt like I was messed up and I definitely didn't have my act together to be teaching or spreading anything, let alone the gospel. But somewhere in my mind, I knew that God used flawed, blemished, wrinkled people. I was very familiar with Paul and his life story. I knew about several other broken people and situations throughout history where God showed up and got the glory, but surely, he didn't mean he would use *me*! He could not possibly want to extend grace to *me*! It wasn't until I heard his still voice. It was when I heard the whistle. God showed me something very important. I discovered that it was *because* of my flaws, my spots, my wrinkles, my mistakes, my blemishes, that He uses me. Not in spite of them.

Which of these are yours? Which of these have you been thinking about giving up or giving in? Like Paul, like me, and yes, even *you* have been chosen by God to be used, because it is in that weakness, that brokenness, those blemishes, wrinkles, and/or deepest end of the ocean that God manifests a voice to reach others who may be feeling like they don't measure up to being used by God. God wants us to reach those very people that are feeling like their mistakes render them unusable, or that they have gone too far out into the deep darkness and can't have a relationship with him. The Bible is a clear example that God didn't use perfect people. Like me, they weren't even in the ballpark, so they definitely weren't in the game. After all, have you investigated those disciples? He used *all* of them, so I know he can use *me*. Yes, Evangelist Staci found herself in a state of sin because I wouldn't tell the truth about my grief. I jumped into the deep end of the ocean and I stayed there for years, weighed down with anger and pain. Glory to God for looking up. Glory to God for that whistle. Now, my ministry encourages and models the safe space for being transparent about what's going on in my life, and I pour this practice into others. It's better to reach for the life preserver and allow the lifeguard (God) to pull you out than to stay in the deep end of the ocean and drown.

To the reader of this chapter, God can and will use anyone who is *willing* to be used. He used Abraham, who was old; Martha, a worrier; the Samaritan woman, who was divorced multiple times; Rahab, who was a prostitute; Moses, who had speech problems; and David, who was a murderer. Staci was deceitful. Staci was angry. Staci had blemishes. Staci hurt an innocent person. Staci entered into a covenant falsely. The list goes on. Many other people could join this train ride. At the end of the day, God can and will surely use *you* if you surrender those very things that you believe qualify you to be "messed up." In 1 Corinthians 1, it says, "God doesn't call the **QUALIFIED**." It's just like God to choose foolish things in the world to confuse those that believe they are wise and powerful. I encourage you, beloved, look up and listen closely for that whistle to be blown, and then move toward the loving arms of God. No matter what your "it" is, God can use it!

After this thirteen-year deep-end-of-the-ocean experience, I knew that God was *real*. My passport scriptures for this Christian journey were Romans 8:28 and Philippians 1:6. I don't look like what I have been through. God took my flaws, my anger, my brokenness, my deceitfulness, and made all of it work for my good. We tend to believe that the word "all" things implies good things. But make no mistake; God knew what He meant by that word when he breathed it into the writer. He was letting us know that we had to really include every experience, every relationship, every encounter or event into *His* process, and they were going to be used to bring glory to *Him* and make us more dependent on Him, to grow us and strengthen our faith so that we could reach the masses.

We also tend to believe that the timeframe for those "all" things to manifest is on our timetable. We typically believe that we get to control the temperature, the magnitude, and the frequency of those "all" things. Nope! Not so much. Honestly, not at all! His plan. His process. His timing. Philippians 1:6, lets us know that "Being confident of this very thing, that he which hath begun a good work in you will perform it until the day of Jesus Christ." After our brokenness, messiness, you can fill in your own "it," God takes His mighty hands and as we are going through those "all" things, He is making us relatable to those people who are broken, just like us. I can't relate to the person who believes that they are perfect and forgot that we all have sinned and fallen short of God's glory (Romans 3:23). But I can relate to someone who has lost their parents. I can relate to the person that can't see the residual impact of not being honest about their emotional state. Every situation that I experienced on that cruise of self-destruction showed me how detrimental it is to let go of God's unchanging hands. I learned that if I let go of His hands I am destined to drown. Especially when I let go, and because of grace, He reaches down to grab my hands, and I refuse to take his.

I am here today and able to share my story only for the grace of God. Make no mistake about this. Staci can't take the credit for nothing. God started this work in me and through me, and I will continue to avail myself to be used. I wrestled after God still allowed me to be licensed as an evangelist and to continue on in ministry. I felt like I was such an embarrassment to Him. What He showed me was that He started a good work in me. Souls were still waiting for me and His plan was going to be fulfilled. This journey has humbled me so much. My faith is stronger. I am better. I am wiser. I desire more of Him, and I desire to do more for Him. I thought that my witness would be impacted. God turned this whole journey around. I am ministering more now than I did before I jumped into the deep end of the ocean. God has shown me and the world that if He called me, flawed, broken, blemished, and all, *He* will equip me. As long as I am willing and have a desire to do God's work, then He will continue to "Look at me and make something beautiful out of my life."

So if you are feeling hopeless, messed up, unworthy, unusable or any negative feelings that the enemy wants you to feel, take it from me: God definitely uses messed-up folks, and He will use you, too! Confess that "it." Genuinely turn from "it" and run back into the arms of the one who can present you faultless before HIS presence of his glory with exceeding joy (Jude 1:24). He has the power, the majesty and dominion both now and ever (Jude 1:25) to turn your mess into a message, your problems into praise and your test into testimonies. Just as God has a plan for me, He also has a plan for you.

ABOUT THE AUTHOR

Evangelist Staci has served in ministry at the Beloved Baptist Church in Philadelphia, Pennsylvania since 2008 under the leadership of Pastor Edward and Lady Donna Duncan, Jr. She is a licensed Evangelist, Instructor for the New Discipleship Training Classes, and Coordinator of the Women's Department. She is a co-author of *When Doves Cry Stories That Heal* and of, *Beauty For Ashes: Messages of Hope An Anthology*.

She earned a Bachelor's Degree in Social Relations from Cheyney University and a Master's Degree in Health Administration from the University of Phoenix. She recently graduated from New Life Bible Institute Missionary Training School and now serves on the faculty at the North Campus.

Evangelist Staci has worked in the Child Welfare System for the past 26 years and currently serves as the Operations Director for Child and Family Services at the Philadelphia Department of Human Services.

Staci La`Marr is the proud mother of an adult daughter, Myaah Monique (25) who is her best accomplishment. She is a graduate of Shippensburg University and a Master's Degree candidate at Temple University.

She has tried and has proof that Romans 8:28 and Philippians 1:6 are spiritual seeds that have produced the fruits that are manifesting in her life.

MESSAGE OF HOPE 4

IT ALL WORKS

JENNELL MADDOX

And we know that in all things God works for the good of those who love him, who have been called according to his purpose.

— Romans 8:28

Beloved, have you ever experienced a feeling that your life has greater purpose than what you are currently doing with it? Have you ever envisioned yourself desiring to complete a task, that in reality you felt could never be achieved? You feel that way because (you think) it is just too big for you to handle and execute, due to your lack of...confidence, and possibly just a general lack of what I like to call "the know-how." You may ask the question of where you should begin. Have you ever stayed quiet when you had much to say, but you have built up in your mind ("they don't need my opinion or advice")or you feel someone else is better-equipped and could speak instead?

When I think of all of the things that we as servants of Christ could accomplish in life, things that may have been delayed because of our actions, I have now come to the conclusion that one of the reasons these obstacles or smoke screen barriers exist is because of fear.

Fear can halt the progression of our outcome as productive individuals. Fear often paralyzes us, and can debilitate our progression. An American/Australian evangelist, Nick Vujicic, identifies fear by this acronym:

- False
- Evidence
- Appearing
- Real

Fear is a smoke screen that has the propensity to ultimately cloud our judgment and decision-making skills. So, you may say, what exactly is fear? Fear can be identified by anything that would cause you to become stagnate, unproductive, and immobile; as in, a paralytic state. Fear can also cause you to run. You might ask what you'd be running from. Well, when fear controls your life, there are walls of self-doubt that are built up that would cause a person to feel as if they are incapable or inferior. When opportunities present themselves, you may tend to back down, walk away from them, or just be silent.

Think of 'run' in this manner: When we operate in fear, we Recede, causing us to move backwards. As a result, we become Unproductive in life endeavors. In addition, we operate with a view of everything through the Negative lens.

- Recede (Backwards)
- Unproductive
- Negative (Lens)

Now, let's talk this out. When we recede, we back away from opportunities presented to us. Oftentimes, we build up walls within us that we can't even detect. We make excellent, intelligent excuses as to why we can't do something, when really our fear has developed from a lack of self-confidence that we don't even realize exists.

Oftentimes, we are the ones who will genuinely live our lives pointing out and promoting others to those opportunities. In a pure sense of who you are, you really want to help others, but you don't realize those opportunities have passed you by, and while others move on you remain stagnate and unproductive (R.U.N.). And all the while, the world around you evolves. All because subtly, fear is at work. Due to the fear, you live a life constantly deflecting, cocooning, and receding. You have built walls in your thinking that tell you that someone else is better suited for the job than you (F.E.A.R.). Just as the Bible declared that the enemy is cunning and subtle. Hey, but don't you even worry. Remember, all things work.

You see, that negative lens begins with your thought life and what voice you lend your ear to. Even in this, we must remember Romans 8:28: All Things Work Together for our Good. Let's pause and remember what the scriptures say, because when we fear a seat at a table, we must remind ourselves what the scriptures tell us: Psalm 56:3-4 (ESV)"When I am afraid, I put my trust in you. In God, whose word I praise, in God I trust; I shall not be afraid. What can flesh do to me?"

Fear can come in so many forms. One important form is the fear of your own voice. Oftentimes when a person is operating in fear, there is a tendency toward a subtle feeling deep inside, that what you may say will not be as intelligent as what the next person might say. There may be a subtle feeling deep inside that your comment in a conversation may not be correct, so you remain silent. You are ultimately afraid of the power behind what you have to say (because it really is anointed),so you recede and remain silent. Also, you may be an introvert and your thoughts and comments to a conversation arise after loads of comments have gone back and forth, and you make up your mind that your comment is no longer important in that moment (smoke screen). That level of fear is a fear of rejection. You are fearful of the opinions of others. Beloved. the Bible states in 2 Timothy 1:7 "God has not given us the spirit of fear but of power, love, and a sound mind. This is the point in your life where you find the strength in Christ to realize who *you* are in Christ. Do you know who your Father is? He has got your back. You see, one of my favorite characters in the bible is Elijah. He was a prophet who described himself as one who had served the Lord as well as he could. As for some background content, King Ahab of Israel was married to queen Jezebel. King Ahab and Jezebel chose to worship Baal, who was a pagan god. Jezebel was known for killing the prophets of God as a brutal way to suppress anyone who had the courage to publicly worship Him. Elijah made several attempts to get King Ahab to repent. Eventually, Elijah did what God asked him to, and it resulted in Jezebel putting a decree out in the land to have Elijah killed. Guess what? He got scared. He became fearful of the power of his voice and the power in his stance for the will of God he produced in the land. It got a response.

So what did he do in that very moment of weakness? He forgot who had his back. He forgot who he was in God, and so he hid in a cave (R.U.N). God spoke to him in the cave and asked him, "Elijah why are you here?"

So I say to you, beloved, that God is saying to you... Why are you in this hidden place when there is so much God wants to use you for? Take your stance, remember who you are, and know that God has amazing plans for your life. No matter what roads we travel, get to a solid place in Christ. God will use it to help bring someone else out through you! So again: Beloved why are you running?

Hey, so now that the enemy is exposed, the smoke has cleared and Blinders are off; what should we do now? Well I say it's time to heal, reboot and rebuild. What is the Solution? Build a solid foundational relationship in Christ. This is the time for you to realize who God is in your life and who you are in him.

- Rev: 1:8: He is the alpha and the omega the beginning and the end.
- Galatians 3:5: He is a miracle-working God.
- Jeremiah 32:17, 27: He is all powerful.
- Psalm 139 :1, 13: He is ever present.
- Numbers 23:19: He is unchangeable.
- Hebrews 13:5: He is never leaving us or forsaking us.
- Isaiah 53:5: He is our healer.
- Romans 11:20: He is our deliver.
- As you walk through overcoming fear, you must speak the word over your life in the form of positive affirmation. Remind yourself what the word of God says about you!
- We are loved by God.
- We are forgiven.
- We are delivered.
- We are healed by his stripes.
- We are free from fear.
- We are heirs of eternal life.
- We are joint heirs with Christ Jesus.
- We are being transformed by the renewing of our minds.

When you are at your wits' end and are at a point of weakness, remember who you are in Him. Listen, beloved: Fear has the propensity to become a distraction. I am somewhat swayed by the ideology that we are too easily distracted by what we hear. When subtle negativity is being presented to our thought life, it is so easy to believe that negative voice, to the point that it is all you hear. That voice has built the lens of life you operate from. Sadly, though, when we only hear negative thoughts, we unknowingly tune out the voice of our Lord and savior, Jesus Christ.

Maybe part of the problem is that we must work on our relationship with the Lord Jesus so that we are in tuned with the positive affirmations He speaks to us daily, which can be found is his word: Matthew 6:11 "Give Us this day Our Daily Bread"(selah).

A solid relationship with Christ is the key to overcoming any form of adversity. When we fill our minds with the word of God, we are consistently being transformed as our mind renews in Him. The Bible tells us in Ephesians 6:12 that we wrestle not against flesh and blood but against principalities. Our mind could be the enemy's battlefield if we allow him access. The moment we accept seeds of self-doubt, it continues to manifest.

Imagine this, as I would like to use imagery for a moment: Imagine your mind being enveloped by a balloon. Yes, I said a balloon. The acceptance of a seed of self-doubt acts as if your mind has been encapsulated by this balloon. The balloon represents a stronghold. Each moment you accept negative words about yourself, the enemy blows air into that balloon, allowing it to inflate. Remember, your mind is inside the balloon, as this is a stronghold over your mind. The enemy is holding on to the end of that balloon so that nothing escapes—not air and not even the negative thought he just planted. So with your mind encapsulated in the stronghold, those negative thoughts are having a field day, developing subtly each day. Those negative thoughts remain because they have not escaped, but have an opportunity to morph into more negativity, further developing this ideology of fear and self-doubt.

In your own strength, with an undeveloped relationship with God, when you try to fight the fear, that balloon (stronghold) acts as a barrier, because in your own strength, you are not strong enough to combat the enemy. The moment we begin to read our daily bread, the word of God, the Ruach (the very breath of God) begins to take action. God fights on your behalf as He removes the hand of the enemy off of your mind. As you read His word, God blows into that balloon (onto the stronghold, new breath combating all negativity until that balloon, or stronghold, is broken and you are free in Christ Jesus).

So I ask the question: How much one-on-one time do you set aside for God? (Selah)

I can remember a time in my life where I was completely devoted to studying the word of God. I mean, I had pages upon pages of notes from my personal studies, notes from sermons I had heard and analyzed over the years. I felt the spirit of God upon my life as if we were one. I did not move without His consultation, without ensuring every step I took was backed up by His word. I felt empowered by Him, and strong and confident. Hey, Jesus really was my BFF. Then life happened and I became subtly engulfed in work, hobbies, friendships, etc., and slowly but surely, those study times dwindled (and hey, I didn't even realize). Before I knew it, I reduced studying God's word to Saturday mornings and Sunday morning sermons, and then it happened: This once-confident young lady began to second-guess everything she ever did in life.

The one thing that remained the same for me was my prayer life. I remained consistent in prayer. However, I was then faced with the reality that even though I was praying consistently, I could not hear God's direction or correction because I allowed negative thoughts to enter in (remember that balloon). It created a stronghold. If God was speaking to me, I could not hear Him over my negative thinking because I was not allowing His daily bread, His Word to bring new life and elevated thinking.

I realized that was the problem: It is so very easy to accept and believe something negative about yourself. But remember who you are, beloved; you are God's chosen, you are loved and cherished by Him. When God created you, beloved, he said, "And it is good!" (Hey, there is no negativity in that!)

We must declare from this moment: I will not recede. No more backing away. I will stand in confidence. I will not be unproductive anymore. I will be productive with my time and talent. I will not allow negativity. No more negative thoughts about myself.

> *Philippians 4:13: I can do all things through Christ, who strengthens me.*

So now that we have made our declaration, let's begin to take this walk into a life of freedom! Remember, beloved, John 8:36: "Whom the son sets free is free indeed."

You may ask the question: Where do I go from here? Where do I start? Well, beloved, let's map out your steps to freedom. Let's be reminded that the scriptures tell us: "Man shall not live by bread alone, but by every word that proceeds out of the mouth of God." (Matthew 4:4)The word "proceeds" speaks to the fact that what comes from the mouth of God is in the present tense. It is current and active and continual. His word is alive. This is one of the reasons working on building your active prayer and study life is important to building a solid foundation to combat fear and any other negative thinking that may try to come your way. Beloved, remember that prayer and study go hand in hand. They are solid foundational partners. Imagine pouring cement on a housing foundation. Cement is a composite of:

I. A chemical combination (your prayers to God's ears)

2. Raw rock material(i.e. limestone) (The Word of God; solid rock is strong enough for anything. Together, they build a structure on which we stand. Remember, your prayers keep you in fellowship with God and the word is like a two-edged sword it cuts through anything the enemy may come to try you with. Beloved, when you have the word in you, that is the only thing we can use to combat the enemy.)

Remember Jesus in the wilderness. Let's take a look:

"4 Then Jesus was led by the Spirit into the wilderness to be tempted[a] by the devil. 2 After fasting forty days and forty nights, he was hungry. 3 The tempter came to him and said, "If you are the Son of God, tell these stones to become bread."

4 Jesus answered, "It is written: 'Man shall not live on bread alone, but on every word that comes from the mouth of God.'[b]"

5 Then the devil took him to the holy city and had him stand on the highest point of the temple. 6 "If you are the Son of God," he said, "throw yourself down. For it is written:

"He will command his angels concerning you,

and they will lift you up in their hands,

so that you will not strike your foot against a stone.'[c]"

7 Jesus answered him, "It is also written: 'Do not put the Lord your God to the test.'[d]"

8 Again, the devil took him to a very high mountain and showed him all the kingdoms of the world and their splendor. 9 "All this I will give you," he said, "if you will bow down and worship me."

10 Jesus said to him, "Away from me, Satan! For it is written: 'Worship the Lord your God, and serve him only.'[e]"

11 Then the devil left him, and angels came and attended him."

Beloved, it was only when Jesus spoke the word over the enemy's taunting that the enemy was defeated. In your prayer life, beloved, begin to speak the word of God over each negative thought and feeling and you will see that the enemy will flee. Beloved, remember that it is a process. Spending time with God and His word are the relationship builders needed. Beloved, when we read the word of God, it activates our faith. Hey, it reminds me of the popular saying that we see all over t-shirts: "Faith over Fear." Well, it is something to live by. That saying, is also what helps to remind me who I was in Christ, and that I don't have to walk in fear. God did not create fear, but He gave us power! Beloved, we have the authority. Fear is a mere illusion, because it was already defeated at the cross. I remember a time when I allowed fear to rise up and a dear sister/friend of mine sent me a gift by mail. It was a shirt that stated: "Faith Over Fear." You see, she had no idea the struggles I was struggling with, because I didn't share. Beloved, I know firsthand that fear is this internal battle. Receiving that gift reminded me of the relationship I built with the Lord. He cared about so much that He inspired her to purchase that shirt, and to her, it may have been just a thoughtful gift. To me, however, it was God's personal message as a reminder that He sees me, He cares, and He loves me dearly. That simple gesture helped me to keep going. Beloved, this writing is a tool to help you to keep going, keep praying, keep studying, and keep believing. Remember, beloved, that all things work together for your good.

So, beloved, that nagging idea you have—that business plan, that book, that upgrade in your job position you have been wanting to take (yes all of that and more)—go forth and just do it. Because you can, in Jesus' name. God gave you the vision, beloved. Hey, make it plain. (Habakkuk 2:2) The best place to be in life, beloved, is in the will of God, doing what He anointed and appointed you to do.

You see, any thought or idea that has positive endings, but seems too big, that's the one. That idea that seems like it would take you out of the cocoon you are in, that's the one. That program idea that you know would bless millions, but you are scared, terrified, and afraid? Yes, that is the one. Beloved, what are you afraid of? Is it yourself? Does the image of your greatness scare you? Or is it something else, like the opinions of others? I have been there. All of the above. You see, I have been there. I used to downplay my own intelligence because I was afraid of saying something that someone would think was inarticulate or unintelligible, and the thought of someone thinking that was excruciating. So, I stayed silent a lot!

At times, when in the midst of a conversation or an interactive lecture or any setting where it required me to voice my thoughts and opinions, I would have the answer to a question or an opinion but, in that brief, moment fear would rear its ugly head and I would think to myself, *If I say that, they will think less of me.*

Beloved, I had to search within myself to figure out how fear got a hold of me, and that search that took years to develop. Then it clicked; I remembered myself as a young student in the second grade. My teacher at the time would do spontaneous open quizzes. All of the students would have to get up and make a huge circle around the perimeter of the classroom. She would call on us one by one and ask a question, and we were instructed to step forward when answering the question. If we knew the answer, we stepped back in line. If not, we sat at our desk. I remembered my name being called and stepping forward to answer her question, and I vividly remember that the answer I gave her was incorrect. She proceeded to embarrass me in front of my entire class.

She said, "You should have known that answer. Do you have a learning disability? Are you dyslexic?"

I was mortified and utterly hurt. Now, most people would think that my classmates would laugh and snicker, but you couldn't hear a pin drop. My classmates were silent as I took my seat. That silence seemed like it lasted a lifetime. The test continued on without me. The fact that my classmates said nothing was the worst experience, because I didn't know what they were thinking of me in terms of my intelligence, my character, and my appearance. Beloved, I was eight, and it took a lifetime to develop into this life of running and cocooning. I always thought that it may have been easier to hear the laughing or snickering. I may have compartmentalized it differently, rather than developing this internal smoke screen of being fearful of what others may be thinking of me.

I encourage you to find where fear was able to attach itself to your mind, and deal with it from the root. Beloved, reliving this story brought tears to my eyes, because it took me years to deal with how that moment broke my spirit. I did not realize the impact it had on my life and the decisions I made over the years because of it. I was too young then to think that I actually never forgave her. Once I realized my root story, I cried (which is okay, because that is where healing can begin), and then forgave her so that I could be released.

Beloved, find your root story. Everyone's origin story is different. I know I made a choice to find out where fear began in my life and how it developed silently over the years. You see, beloved, self-care is very important. I had to learn that the hard way, after years of deflecting and paying attention to everyone except myself took a toll on me as I became depleted. Beloved, take a moment (Selah), reflect, and regroup. It is time to take your life back from the hand of the enemy. Beloved, God promised us beauty out of the pile of ashes that came from the myriad of bad decisions we have made in life. Just know, beloved, that someone else needs to hear your story and how you overcame all of the vicissitudes of life. Beloved, remember that all things work together for your good; no matter what happens, God will work it out for you. So, beloved, no more running. No more receding. No more days of unproductivity. No more days of negative thinking. You will, however, give your mind, body, and spirit a daily dose of God's word as you study to reconnect with God. You will commit to an increased prayer life as you pray the word of God over your life, reminding yourself who God is and who you are in Him.

In Jesus' Name Beloved I know you will overcome Fear as long as you remember God's got you. You will realize that beauty will come from ashes Just as God has promised. Most people when you consider ashes you may think it is useless but beloved it is not. There are many ways to use burnt ashes. You See Beloved ashes such as wood ash can be used as a fertilizer for soil allowing your garden to thrive. (remember all things Work) Beloved all of the difficulties you have faced in life or bad decisions they become the ashes needed to fertilize all of your gifts and talents. It's time Beloved, you can Do this through Christ as we declare beauty out of our lives. I am praying for you beloved. (IT ALL Works)!

ABOUT THE AUTHOR

Rev. Jennell Maddox has been an ordained Reverend since 2008. Rev. Jennell Maddox received a Bachelor's degree in Business Administration from Eastern University. She also received a Diploma in Pastoral Studies from Palmer Seminary's Eastern School of Christian Ministry. Currently, Rev. Jennell Maddox is pursuing a Master of Divinity at *Palmer Theological Seminary*.

Called to pastoral ministry, Rev. Jennell has pastored youth for over eight years. Youth ministry is the highlight of her ministerial career. She has served in the missionary capacity for several local organizations. In fact, Rev. Jennell Maddox is the Founder of *Koinonia Life Ministries* whose aim is to serve those who are part of the homeless community. She has partnered with many organizations and has led many youth short-term missionary outreaches both local and across the United States. She has had the esteemed opportunity to serve in the City of Tijuana in Mexico which was a life-changing experience that informed and inspired how she decided to structure *Koinonia Life Ministries*.

Rev. Jennell is also a Therapeutic Recreation Director. She utilizes her artistic skills as a therapeutic regimen for individuals who suffer from Alzheimers and Dementia. Rev. Jennell Maddox has worked in the Therapeutic Recreational field for over 16 years, enhancing the life of seniors living in long term care facilities. Upon graduating with an MDiv, Rev. Jennell Maddox will enroll in the

Doctorate Degree Program at Eastern University where her field of Study will be Marriage and Family Counseling.

Rev. Maddox stands on the Word of God. Her favorite verse is Romans 8:28.

All things work together!

MESSAGE OF HOPE 5

To My Niece,

Thanks for always being sooo kind
& thoughtful. You are such a
sweetheart. I miss those crazy
& fun days over Joe's with you
guys.

Thanks for the love & support.
I really appreciate you.

I love you

MY PAST GAVE ME A PATH TO THE FUTURE

KELLI M. GRAY

"There is always light, if only we're brave enough to see it-if only we're brave enough to be it."

— Amanda Gorman

Education about adult sex offenders and sex itself is important for children because they will have little if any knowledge of why or what has happened to them. Shame is a predominant feature of the child's response to abuse (Knauer, 2000, p 74-82).

There was a little black girl who lived with her mother, younger brother, uncle (godfather), and uncle's girlfriend. The little black girl was me. It was the Seventies. Her mother and father were separated and eventually divorced. This little girl cherished the ground her daddy walked on. He called her "princess." Princess knew she was very special to him. Princess always looked beautiful; her parents made sure of that. Princess didn't want her parents to get divorced. When they divorced, living with her mother was just fine, but sadly, she was separated from her daddy.

That was a turning point in the little black girl's life. The little black girl is me, the writer. She was a sweetheart and had a kind soul, but all of that was about to change for the worse.

When she was nine years old, the little girl met a real-life devil. He was probably about thirty-five years old. When they met, this girl lived in Germantown, a neighborhood in Philadelphia. On her street, on the same side on which she lived, lived the monster. He was a family friend who visited her family's home often. His parents were friends with the little girl's grandmother, who she calls Gram. The little girl was the oldest granddaughter.

The monster was a sexual predator. While she can't remember exactly when or how the horrible acts started, she knows that they lasted for several years and that she was between nine and thirteen years old. The little girl thinks that the only reason the sexual abuse stopped is because she wasn't precious and beautiful anymore. She wasn't a princess anymore.

Over time, she came to feel less and less valued, and even began to think she was ugly. She had started to become a monster, too.

The abusing devil never penetrated her, but made the little girl perform oral sex on him. He even made her look at Playboy magazines and watch him jerk off. The first time he ejaculated, after forcing her mouth on him, she asked, "What's that?" in the midst of choking. The devil told her that it was his love for her.

When she got to middle school, he came, too. When he picked her up from school, her friends thought he was her uncle. That was what he told the little one to tell them. When he gave her money, he told her to share the money with her friends so they would be nice to her. She was an excellent student. In fact, she was sometimes called the teacher's pet, and that worked for her, but eventually, the little girl got to the point that she didn't want to go to school anymore.

On Tuesdays, the devil was scheduled to pick her up from school. As often as possible, the little girl would ask her teacher if she could go to the bathroom before the school bell rang. Her teacher would always let her go. The little girl didn't really have to go to the bathroom. Instead, she'd use a different exit to leave the school and go home. She knew where he would be coming from and was able to avoid seeing him. Still, the sexual abuse didn't stop.

She never told anyone. Why, you might ask, didn't she tell? The devil constantly threatened to kill her mother, father, and godfather if she told. He knew that they were the three most special people in her life. His threat terrified the child. If they were killed, who would love and take care of her?

The devil was a fat man. He only wore cotton sweatsuits that were green, black, and blue, and he always wore a tan trench coat. Always. He always smelled sweaty. He always drove a green Volkswagen. And his bedroom, which was on the third floor of the house he lived in, was always messy and stinky. He lived with his parents.

Gram's three girlfriends lived on the devil's block. They were very nosy neighbors. Since the little girl wasn't allowed to tell on her abuser, she thought for sure that the nosy girlfriends would see her going inside his home, or that they would see her talking to him and say, "Rosie (that is Gram's name), what's that child doing over at the devil's house?

But they never did.

The little girl felt that no one helped or loved her. Even when she started to act out, her family members had no idea what she was enduring.

She thinks the monster finally stopped because the little girl wasn't as innocent anymore. He would see her playing with her friends. He knew that she'd grown a little reckless and that she talked a lot, so she guessed that he'd decided, "I can't take that chance anymore, she might tell."

But she didn't.

I know, because the little girl was me.

My hair was short and very coarse. Today, people would love that texture hair, but back then, nope. I was a just a lost little nappy-headed girl who needed a perm every six to eight weeks. I was brown-skinned and I was built like my paternal grandmother, with shapely legs and a plump backside. I had small breasts, though. One time, I was riding my brother's big wheel with a tube-top on. The top fell off without me knowing and the neighborhood boys laughed and teased me for a while. "We saw those little black dots," they taunted. The teasing was so bad that I stayed in the house and watched The Flintstones and The Brady Bunch until I wasn't teased anymore.

I learned to fight well, and my girl cousins my age always got me to fight their battles. In the summer, I was always at my cousin's house back up Haines Street. In the Germantown section in Philly, the communities were broken down by neighborhoods (Pulaski Town, Haines Street, Summerville, Dog Town, and Brick Yard). My family lived in Pulaski Town, but then my mother, brother, and I moved to Summerville. One time, my cousins wanted me to fight this girl, though I can't remember why. I beat her up inside her house and then dragged her outside and did the same thing. I was praised for that horrible action. I was still a little lost girl, but by that time, I had become a teenager, and I was getting in trouble. I stole money from the adults, lied, had a bad attitude, and cried a lot. But people never saw that last part.

My senior year of high school, I had math with some 11th graders. My classmate told me that three girls were going to do me like the movie *Carrie* and throw paint on me at the prom. Why? Because they hated me, and I was talking to one of the girls' boyfriend. I wasn't really in trouble in school. As I stated earlier, I was a teacher's pet. Some of my classmates didn't like that, because I could really do what I wanted. I did my schoolwork on top of it. My classmate, a junior, was worried for me, but I told her not to worry. I never told a soul, and I always keep a secret. I knew I could handle it. How, I don't know, but it just had to happen.

I was sharp on my prom, but was willing to get messed up.

I took an ex-boyfriend from Logan, a section in Philly. I never told him what was supposed to happen, but if he had known, he would have been down for anything. He said he loved me. He was murdered when he was nineteen years old. Before I told him yes about going to my prom, he and his mother were upset because I hadn't asked *him* yet. Another ex-boyfriend asked could he go with me to prom, and I told him yeah, but my prom date had his mother call me and ask why he wasn't going. I told him that if he'd gotten his mother to call me, I would let him go, because I knew he still loved me. I never told the other ex until two weeks before the prom. I kept letting him think he was going, which was just evil and unfair. When I finally told him, he and his mother were pissed at me for a long time. Bad karma did follow me though, but not to my prom. Those girls didn't do anything, because they knew what was best for them. We had a great time at the prom.

My mother said I was always a good girl, and she didn't know what happened to me. I will tell you: anger, hatred, and self-hate. I treated people wrong because that little girl wanted to be free. I was free from the sexual abuse, but not mentally. Never in a million years did my mother think I had been abused in that horrible, horrible way.

A great deal of research indicates a strong relationship between being abused by a parent and/or witnessing inter-parental violence as a child and being violent toward a partner as an adult (Astin et al.,1995; Barnett and Hamberger, 1992; Jouiles and Norwood 1995).

Forgive your abuser, so you can move on. I didn't say forget. Forgiveness *helps you* move on to a road of recovery.

SADNESS, SURPRISES & SURVIVAL

When I gave birth to my twin daughters, I did not want my children to go through what I went through. I always told them that if someone says they are going to harm me, it's not true. Tell, please tell. I want to keep you safe and I will do anything in my power to do just that. People like to scare and manipulate people, especially children, and keep them helpless.

The fact that they were girls was significant, and twins! Wow!!

I lived through my daughters, their entire lives. When they were children, I was so overprotective. They are adults now, and I'm the same way. Vacations that I didn't take as a child, I took my daughters. Most vacations, it was just us. We still take vacations each year. If I had one dollar, I broke it down for us, 33 percent each. I never slighted them. We shared everything. People would love to see them and always wanted to see what they had on. I kept them sharp every day. They always looked like they were coming from a photo shoot, even on the weekends.

They depended on me, and I was right there for them. I didn't really hang out much, anymore. If I didn't have the money for something, I made a call (my mom, Gram, and or my uncle/godfather) and they looked out for us. I stayed home for sixteen months when they were born, quit my insurance job (customer service), and collected welfare to make sure we had the money we needed.

I met my twins' father when he was sixteen years old, in the late Eighties. I was three years older than he was. We dated almost three years. I worked at Rite-Aid and he and his dad had a stand outside of Rite-Aid, selling Islamic items (oil, papers, incense, etc.). He lived with his paternal aunt. Our relationship was on and off. I was close to his parents, siblings, and other family members. I did deal with hustlers. This one was smooth, dark, and handsome. We had verbal altercations and one physical fight, though I think I started them all. We dressed alike, and my mother liked him very much. The last six months of our relationship, I thought we were good. We talked about moving in together and even looked at two apartments. We went to Wildwood, NJ, for the weekend for some fun in the sun, as we had done two years prior.

But this time, he appeared a little distant. I thought it was because he was trying to leave the street life completely alone. He enrolled in nursing school; he was a smart dude. I never knew what was bothering him, but I made the best of our time together.

That Monday, he stated that he was upset because his father wouldn't let him borrow his car to come see me. His car was in the shop. Usually, I would have gotten upset if he couldn't come see me, but that time, I knew he was coming to my job to see me the next day. He always came to see me at work, at an insurance company in downtown Philly. On that day, I wanted to tell him something, but didn't want to do it over the phone. I wanted to see his face and reaction.

But Tuesday came and went with no communication from him, and that had become unusual in our relationship. I kept beeping him 911, but no response. I was pissed. I called his mom, who I was very close to. If anyone knew where he was, she would. But this time, she said she hadn't talked to him. I was getting worried, and called her twice a day for an update, but she didn't have one. It was now Thursday, and the last time I spoke to him was Monday. I called his mother's house, knowing she was at work but that someone would be at their house.

This time, a female answered and asked who I was. I told her, and she cursed me out and told me not to call his house again.

I wasn't angry. I was confused. I immediately called his mother at work and told her what had happened, and she said it was her niece. "You know she plays too much. I will talk to her about that," she said. I did know her niece and that she did play a lot, but I hadn't recognized her voice. I knew I was his girlfriend, and wasn't worried about any other chick.

At that time, I had two besties. They both told me that he would show up and not to worry. But my birthday was on Saturday and this dude had always been with me on my birthday. He never missed a birthday, and we planned them together. My 21st birthday was powerful. We rented a limo and dined at The Chart House, an upscale restaurant overlooking the water. Another birthday, he brought me a herringbone necklace with a diamond. These gifts were great when you were young in the late Eighties and early Nineties.

But on this birthday, we hadn't talked about what we were doing. My birthday came, my mother went birthday shopping, and my immediately family threw me a house party. I called his house on my birthday morning and his mother answered, sounding tired. I asked her if she was asleep, and she just said my name.

I lost it. I knew my man was gone from this earth. He was missing for four days. A man walking his dog and looking for aluminum cans found his decomposing body. He was only nineteen years old. That late August sun was very hot, and his mouth and hands had been taped. He was shot eight to ten times and twice in the head. He had his money on him, but no ID. His identity was confirmed through dental records.

This couldn't be. *God I'm trying to be a good girl, I am. Why?* I never told him I was pregnant. Yes, pregnant and now alone. What a combination. We went to his house soon after I got the news. His mother said, "I need to tell you something, because you are getting ready to find out. He was having a baby with someone else. She is three months pregnant and is on her way here."

Me and my mother looked at each other, and I didn't say a word. I took all this information in. She did come, and wanted to fight me. It was going to happen, but we were pulled apart. She was pissed because in the obituary she was called the mother of his unborn child and I was called a very special loved one. However, this dude was living a double life, and he never told me about any of this. That was why he was distant in Wildwood. That girl knew all about me, but when she saw pictures, she thought I was his cousin.

In my world, his family betrayed me. I learned that he had been living with his unborn child's mother. But he was with me and said he wanted to move in with me. Every time he left my mom's house, he would call me about twenty-five minutes later. It took about twenty minutes to get from my home to his mother's, and if he didn't call me in thirty minutes, I was calling him. But since he was living with this girl, he would make sure he called me. He didn't want me to call his mother's house, because then his family would have to lie to me. The truth was, he didn't live there anymore.

That evening, I told my two best friends that I thought I was pregnant. One said, "I know." The other said, "No, you are not. You just want to be pregnant because that girl is pregnant." Her comment stung, and I felt betrayed again. Then it was confirmed I was pregnant, and with twins! No way! Yes way!

My first trimester was a trip. I would bleed every other week and was constantly going to my doctor. One afternoon, my doctor came in the room and said, "Listen, I'm tired of this. I know your boyfriend was murdered, but you better get yourself together. Do you want an abortion?"

I told him I absolutely didn't.

"Then you'd better straighten up. Your babies can feel what you are going through, and if they come out with some deformities, it'll be your fault. I'm stepping out of the room and will give you time to think about it. I need to know what you are going to do."

Someone else might have thought that was unprofessional, but I needed to hear that. I got my coo-coo self together and had a set of healthy twins with a vaginal birth. Domonique and Monique Fields Gray, though we called them Dee and Mo. They were a little angry at me that they didn't have a girly middle name (I had given them the middle name of Fields, for their dad). Oh well. I thought when they got married that they would change their last name and Fields would be dropped, though I wanted them to carry Fields forever. He was their father, who they never met. I used to take them to the cemetery, when they were younger, to have lunch and sit there in a chair or a blanket. It sounds crazy, but nope. I needed that. I wanted them to be as close to him as I was.

I was a single mother, and did receive support from my mother and other family members. But I was their mother. I had to set a good example for them. When they were born, I would just stare at them. I couldn't believe I was responsible for these beauties. Yes, God blessed me with these girls, and I was going to try and be the best mother and provider I could be. Since I was a young and single mother (only twenty-two), I didn't put them on punishment when they were younger (from five to eleven), because if they were on punishment, that meant I was on punishment, too. If we had plans, I would spank them and then we would go out. They would look at me like I was crazy. I'd just spanked them, and now we were going to have fun.

Yup, welcome to our world.

SELF-IMPROVEMENT

I decided to face my demons and work on myself so I could be the best for my girls. I finally told some family members about my childhood sexual assault, after twenty years. My dad was now deceased, but my mother was angry and supportive, and helped me deal with my trauma. I finally attended therapy (Trauma-Focused Cognitive Behavioral and Solution-Focused Brief).

One day, we were at a community cookout and the monster came. My heart dropped. I saw my mother going over to him, and though I asked her not to make a scene, she said to the monster, "I know what you did," and walked away. My mother was a firm believer that you would have to answer to your Creator, and she thought the monster had it coming.

He put his head down and left. I just hoped he never violated anyone else, but as sick as he was, I know he did. A few years later, we heard he had a medical issue and died. "You reap what you sow, and karma will come," I thought.

You will be broken for a while, but get support and help. You need it. You can't deal with it alone. Talk to it out and don't keep it hidden, because that's when self-destruction takes the lead (drugs, abusing alcohol, stealing, lying, fighting, abusing sex, and other negative behaviors).

MESSAGES OF HOPE: PART I

BE FEARLESS

What were you afraid of? I always had crazy relationships, because I hated the word 'no' or rejection. The monster who took my innocence and then just stopped being with me was where rejection started, in my mind. I kept asking myself why he didn't love me anymore. Was I ugly? Had he found someone that looked better than me? Was she light skinned, with curly hair? I didn't have any of those traits. *You hurt me and then left, and when I saw you, you acted like nothing ever happened.*

> *"Power's not given to you. You have to take it,"*
> — Beyoncé Knowles Carter

SEEK HELP

You need someone to assist you. You can't do everything by yourself. What worked for me was going to therapy, talking to people I really trusted. Trust others with your story, because everyone is not out to harm you. Give people a chance. Open up. Stop holding things in because when you hold on to anger, you are likely to abuse others in some way. Anger consumes you and you start to backslide.

BE PATIENT

I struggle with patience. If it doesn't happen right now, I don't think it's going to happen. God doesn't like to be rushed. He is always here, but He will show up in His own time.

- Live life to the fullest. Laugh a lot. Be kind. Travel the world. Be grateful. Have faith. Smile more. Worry less. Love with all you heart.

MOVE FORWARD

Looking back held me back.

My first marriage was not for love, but because he was a good man. I knew he could help me raise my daughters. That was a terrible mistake. Never do that. If you don't love someone, don't do it. It wasn't fair to him or my daughters. It was very cruel. Dee and Mo's father is not on this earth, and I know he would be a great father. How was I supposed to do this? Before I had a stable car, I would push them in their stroller on the avenue. As I stated earlier, people loved to see how they were dressed. People would come up to us and say how pretty they were. There were two incidents when men came up to them and said how cute they were. The first time, Mo said, "Are you my father?" He looked, and I was hurt. I thought he was saying to himself that I didn't even know who their father was. I didn't say anything to the girls, but it happened again. I was hurt again, and thought the same thing. I did care what people thought of me. My daughters saw all their cousins with fathers, and they were fatherless. They didn't understand, but I couldn't get angry with them. They did have great male role models in their life.

I kept dwelling on why I was abused and why he chose me. I could smell him, see him, hear him. When these things happened, I was headed for destruction, arguing, fighting, and lashing out. I kept asking God why, and He said that I wasn't ready for healing.

If you want to live a productive life and want your children going in the right direction, stop, listen, and act in a positive manner. You are asking for help, now receive it. Get on those knees and pray and walk with your head up. Your past doesn't define you; your negative actions do. Move forward.

HELP OTHERS

"If you don't like something, change it. If you can't change it, change your attitude."

— Maya Angelou

I became a teacher in the charter school system, and now I'm a social worker for children and youth in Philadelphia County. I have been a social worker for over fifteen years. I'm a change agent, helping children and adults learn to break the cycle and try to live a positive and productive lifestyle. I know it's hard. I'm a witness to that. Therapy has helped me cope with life and trauma. The last time I attended therapy was about two years ago. I also talked with my peers, as we share some of the same stories. I'm still working on patience, which I lack. I'm a work in progress. Some of my clients help me get through issues, and they don't even know it.

KEEP FAMILY FIRST

My daughter and I were baptized together. What a great feeling! I never had any other children, despite my twins wanting more siblings. I wanted to give all my time and love to these special gems. It was just us for a very long time. I leaned on them quite often, and they didn't even know it. When they left to go to college, I had anxiety about being alone. I felt alone and rejected again. I had to talk to others. They were not leaving me; they were getting an education and learning how to live without me. But it felt like they were. One twin went to Spelman (Atlanta). I didn't want her to go that far, but she wasn't going to have it any other way. All her schools were outside of Philly, so you would have thought she was running away from me. But that's just her.

She excelled at Spelman and was class president of her senior class (2013). The other twin decided that school wasn't for her at that time. She completed two years at Westchester University. However, she is in school again now, and kicking those grades. Great job, ladies. I have always been my daughters' biggest cheerleader! The sky's the limit, and I will always be there. I never told them no; I said go for it. If it doesn't work, oh well. Try something else. Don't let fear or what someone else says stop you. Take what you want.

One of my twins taught in two different countries for eleven months a piece: Shenzhen, China and Istanbul, Turkey. I visited both places while she was there. She was also in the Peace Corps for twenty-two months, in Guinea, Africa. That was the most powerful experience I have ever had. I was there for thirteen days. I traveled to sixteen countries and seven of them, I visited alone. I traveled to seventeen states in our country. Many of them, I visited seven or more times.

TAKE CARE OF YOURSELF

Self-care-is a must! Read a book, do yoga, travel, use body care, shop if you have the money, go to the movies, or hang with friends. Spa time is the best. I drink socially, get a good night's sleep, and play games. Listen to music. I do all of these; they help the mind, soul, and body.

On April 15, 2021, I was married a second time, in Las Vegas, Nevada. It was my husband's first time on a plane. We love each other very much, though I'm still learning to share my space and my world. It was me and my daughters for over twenty-six years, and now there's someone else. He is a good man. I'm more of a jump-to-it person, where he isn't. We used to see each other when we were in our late teens, but he always had a girlfriend.

"Father, I thank you for having heard me. I knew that you always hear me."

— John 11:41-42

MESSAGE OF HOPE: PART II

1. Heal. Remember what happened to you and learn how to heal from it.
2. Stop dancing with your demons.
3. Perform good deeds for others, and don't tell everyone about it.
4. Turn off the news and social media and meditate.
5. Love yourself. If you don't, no one will.
6. Open up your blinds and let the sunlight shine in.
7. Take a deep breath. Breathe when you are stressed. Each minute will help your body and mind.

FINAL THOUGHTS

I shared my story because I know someone is going through what I went through and suffering in silence. I know how you feel. I want you to realize that you are beautiful. Start believing it. Take care of yourself, brush off your demons. Start a positive relationship with people you trust. Stop wanting to do others wrong as they did you.

I know. I still struggle with that. Be kind, even if they are not kind to you. Let the little things go. Life is short; make the best of it. We all matter in some way or form!

My father died on December 17, 1985, and I still talk with him. I'm still his princess, and I know he is very proud of me. Connect with your past. My past gave me a path to my future.

It is never too late to go to school. I started college in my thirties, my bachelors and master's degrees. I did take six classes for my PhD (psychology), and then had to stop due to financial issues. I plan to go back to school and finish. It doesn't matter when you finish; the prize is that you *do* finish.

> *"As a unique expression of the Divine, I am called to demonstrate the fullness of who I am. Nobody else can do this for me. As I take charge of my time and energy, I am better able to see the beauty in this day, my life and my relationships."*
> — *Daily Word*, Wednesday, January 27, 2021

God's plan for your life far exceeds the circumstances of your day!

Thank you for reading *Message of Hope* and my chapter. Hopefully, we can connect with some of you and bring some positive and helpful tools to help you continue to walk your path. Don't give up; you will get through it. If I made it out of the darkness, so can you. Never stop working on yourself.

There is a light, shine it, shine bright!

ACKNOWLEDGMENTS

pray that you enjoy my story as much as I enjoyed writing it.

Thank you, Delvia, for allowing me to share parts of my life – my messages of hope -- with our readers.

ABOUT THE AUTHOR

Kelli Monique Gray was born and raised in Philadelphia, Pennsylvania. She has lived in Philly her entire life. She is the daughter of Saundra E. and the late James W. Gray, Jr.

Kelli has twin girls, Domonique F. and Monique F. Gray. She's married to Darryl A. Webb whom she wed on April 15, 2017 in Las Vegas.

Her daughters and she were baptized in 2000 at Janes Memorial United Methodist Church, her childhood church. Her daughters are her biggest supporters and her number one cheerleaders. Together, they are her like "The Three Amigos."

Kelli graduated from Germantown High School. Germantown High was an historic institution that existed about 100 years before it closed its doors in 2013 (99 years). She received her associate degree from Community College of Philadelphia (CCP), and her bachelor's and master's degrees from Alvernia University.

Kelli's hobbies are traveling and reading novels. She enjoys walking, riding her bike, yoga and mixed cardio.

MESSAGE OF HOPE

INCARCERATION SAVED ME

KEENAN BISHOP

Before I formed you in the womb, I knew you, before you were
born, I set you apart; I appointed you as a prophet to the nations.
— Jeremiah 1:5

THE BEGINNING

As I look back over my life, I can say God has been with me. I believe God was with me because I had a praying grandmother.

Let me start from the beginning. I was one of six children. Because both of my parents were heroin addicts, we were all raised separately. I was raised by my grandparents. Growing up with drug-addicted parents was a bit confusing for me. My father frequently stayed in the household of my grandparents, and because we had little interaction, it made me feel rejected, although I knew he loved me. We didn't have the typical television father/son relationship, with playing sports, trips to the park trips, and the birds and the bees' conversations, due to the disease of addiction. At the time, I didn't understand the power of addiction and the impact it had on our relationship. This made me feel rejected and unloved by him, but that wasn't the case. The case was that he was sick.

Many people do not understand the disease of addiction and how it is a sickness, but having experienced addiction made me understand my father's behavior. I started to regret the way I acted toward him as a teen, though I'd only acted that way because I didn't understand his struggle at the time.

The other regret I have is that I didn't see my mother before she passed away. I was around nine years old and went with a family friend down on 16th and Catherine and ran into my older brother, Nick. He encouraged me to go to 15th Street to call my mother. After the call, he wanted me to go with him to the projects at 13th Street, and out of fear of getting in trouble, I decided not to go. Looking back, the trouble would have been worth me seeing my mother, because she died not too long after that.

Even through all the pain, struggles, and regret, I know God's hand was on me, because my life could have been a lot worse.

Being raised by my grandparents had its advantages. I was raised as an only child and given a firm Christian upbringing. I had to go to church, whether I liked it or not. I didn't have a choice. I went to good schools and was taken care of by my grandparents. One of the disadvantages was that I lived in fear of my grandparents passing away before I became an adult. They were already retired when I was born, and I feared going into foster care. I was envious of my friends, because their parents were young while my grandparents were elderly.

The point I am trying to get at is that I came from two drug-addicted parents but was nurtured and loved by my grandparents in a Christian home. Eventually, though, nature won over nurture. Many would say that because of my environment, I fell in with the wrong crowd. I hung out in the projects because some of my friends lived there. We stole, sold drugs, robbed people, and conducted burglaries—most of the time, for excitement. I did it for acceptance and because I just didn't care anymore. I wanted to be a part of their crowd, although I was created to stand out. I was not a follower, but this is what some of my friends did. I was on a path to prison, which meant I was going to be a "real man."

THE MIDDLE

There were several things that led to my life spiraling out of control, and one of them was the death of my older brother, Nick, who I idolized. Growing up, I was already kind of troublesome. The night my brother was accidentally killed was the night that my attitude changed. I didn't care about anything or anyone. I became numb to feelings and used things to numb my feelings. I was so hurt by the loss of my brother that it changed everything.

Let me tell the story of how things went down. It was my brother Nick's birthday and we had plans to go to a house party in the projects to celebrate. Some kids from my school were having a party the same night, so I decided to go to that party in West Philly first and meet my brother afterwards.

When I arrived at the projects, there were police everywhere with yellow crime tape, and the crowd was whispering, "You tell him." "No, *you* tell him."

I don't know who told me, but I took off running to Jefferson Hospital. My brother was on life support for a week or two but when the doctors told my family that he was brain dead, they decided to allow Nick to pass on. I thought he was going to make it, because he would squeeze my hand and it looked like he was responding to my touch. But he didn't.

This was a devastating loss for me. By the time I was seventeen years old, I had loss my mother, grandfather, father, brother, and several other significant family members. I was in a lot of pain and could care less about anything and anyone at the time. I wanted to anesthetize my pain, and I did it through drinking, doing drugs, getting high, and violence. My life was spiraling out of control, and I was on a path of destruction. I was acting out because I was in pain and did not know how to address it, other than inflicting more pain on myself and others.

This was where my criminal activity intensified; I robbed, stole cars, and would fight, which eventually led to my conviction and incarceration.

THE TURNAROUND

One day, I called home to talk to one of my daughters. I had been sentenced to go upstate to the penitentiary, and I was going to be leaving that week from the county prison. My oldest daughter, who was six or seven years old at the time, asked me where I was. I told her I was at the cop's house and had to stay there for a while. I said that I couldn't leave and didn't know when I would be coming home. She asked me if I was in jail again, and at that moment I kind of wanted to cry.

That right there was one of the things that made me want to change my life. I was in jail again and hearing my daughter ask me in that way made me feel so bad, emotionally. I felt ashamed and embarrassed, and like I was a failure as a father, especially as my dad had done the same thing to me. I thought to myself, *I need to break this generational curse.*

While in the county, I had begun studying Islam with people I knew from the streets. I was doing it mainly out of curiosity, because my mother and father were both Muslim. They both called me Abdul, because that was what they wanted to name me, but my grandmother, who raised me, called me Keenan. I continued to study Islam until I was sentenced and sent to Camp Hill State Prison. It was at Camp Hill that I had a life-changing experience. It was much like the apostle Paul's Damascus Road experience. I wasn't persecuting Christians and didn't have a conversation with Jesus, but I felt I had betrayed God by studying another religion. One day, I decided to go to church. I was walking to the church and began to cry as I walked. I felt a load was lifting off me. There was a weight removed from me, and I began serving the God my grandmother introduced me to as a child. I began studying the Bible, praying, and attending church services regularly. I felt a sense of peace at this point during my time in prison. I wasn't as worried about too many things. I began to take comfort in God's word: "Therefore do not worry about tomorrow, for tomorrow will worry about itself. Each day has enough trouble of its own. "When I began to attend church and profess to being a Christian, it was not looked upon favorably, but I didn't care what anyone thought. I finally felt free and at peace. The Bible says, "Whom the son sets free is free indeed." My relationship with God was so good at the time that I could rest in a place that was dangerous and chaotic.

While at Camp Hill State Prison, I was put in a cell with an older white guy from Lackawanna County, Pennsylvania. When I was told who my cellmate was, and he came in, I began to size him up. I was a little nervous. He was about six-two and I was only 5'7". He was white. I was black and I was only twenty-one. He looked to weigh close to 300 pounds, and at the time I was maybe about 150. He looked like a mean biker dude, who was probably racist. I was quite sure he perceived me to be a young black thug from the city; a criminal from the projects. I was stereotyping him from what you see or know of a white person that engages in criminal activity. I didn't think we were going to get along, and I didn't want to be in the same cell as him.

But as time went on, we started to develop a friendship. We talked about our families and God, once we found out we had Christianity in common, we got to know each other better. We started having Bible study together and actually became friends. It really made my time in prison go by much smoother and more easily. Our friendship, and my relationship with God, made me more at ease. I wasn't stressed out about going home every day, all day.

This was really just the beginning of my prison stay. I hadn't arrived at my home jail SCI Albion. I started to feel free in my mind and my spirit, and at a certain point we were getting along so well that the guards, noticed we were friends. One day they did a cell search and asked my cellmate if he wanted to be moved away from this nigga. My cellmate told them that he was fine, and from that point on, they treated him like he was one of us, a black person, because of our friendship. Today, that sort of segregation is still going on in the prison system.

For him and me, though, it didn't matter. We did Bible studies and had different conversations about what we would do when we got home and the things we would change. I had decided I was going to go home and live a productive, law-abiding lifestyle and try to raise my kids and take care of my grandma, who was elderly now, but still alive, by the grace of God.

Jim, my cellmate, gave me a pass to get into Heaven to take with me, and told me that when I got there, this would get me in. He made this pass for me because he knew how worried I was. I'd told him about the things I'd done in the past and the lifestyle I'd been living before I came to prison. Jim assured me that God forgives us for our sins. He said he could see that I was a good person and was going to change my life. He said that *that* was what was going to get me into Heaven, but that the pass was a representation of it.

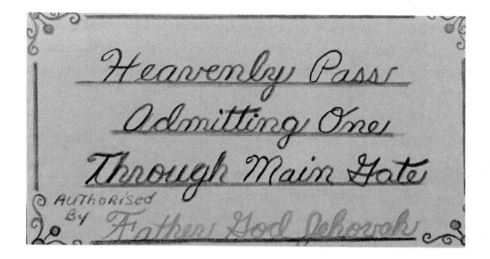

When it was time for me to see the parole board, a few inmates knew I was going up for parole and made statements like that I shouldn't expect to get paroled because they never gave parole inmates the first time around, and I had a violent offense. I was worried, but then I prayed and gave it to God. I told God that if He got me out of this situation, I would turn my life around and not come back to prison.

At the actual hearing, I was doing really well until one of the parole agents began to badger me. I noticed I was getting upset but it was like God tapped me on the shoulder, and my demeanor changed immediately. I began to answer the questions calmly, with eye contact and confidence. I left there a little scared, because the parole agent had said I was a menace to society and asked why I should be granted parole. Those words replayed in my mind for the next eight to ten weeks while awaiting a decision. While pleading and praying to God to be released, I continued to worry.

When the decision came that I was granted parole, I began to thank God for His favor. I made the decision to not tell anyone that I was going home. I just began to make plans for what I was going to do to keep from putting myself in this position again. I was happy to go home but was also afraid. I didn't know what to expect because times had changed, I hadn't been home in a few years.

THE COMEBACK

The day of my release, I didn't tell any family members or friends that I was coming home. I remember showing up at my house and my grandmother answering the door. She first looked through the window, and said, "I know that ain't you." She looked as if she couldn't believe what she was seeing, that I was finally home. When she finally made it to the door, she kept touching my face to see if I was real. She cried out, "Lord Jesus have mercy" and immediately went into praising God for my release and for His protection over my life. I felt relieved that she was happy and there was a joy in our presence. I never told my grandmother how much time I had to do, because she would always make comments about her not making it and being "dead and gone" by the time I came home. My grandmother was very happy to see me, and she immediately started talking about staying out of trouble.

The best part of coming home, besides seeing my family, holding my daughters, and catching up with old friends was having my freedom. I was overjoyed to be free and able to have another shot at life. I was able to take long walks in the morning, smell the different smells of the city, and enjoy something as simple as a cat running across the street. This experience showed me how we take the little things in life for granted: riding a septa bus, fumes from cars, the loud noise in the city, and just regular city smells.

After the initial homecoming, I got to a point where I had to ask myself where I was going to go from here. Spending time in prison saved my life, because I was on a self-destructive path that could have led to my death or the death of someone else. I believe God gave me the prison experience to save me from myself. No matter how far I tried to go, God would not allow me to self-destruct to the point of no return.

Though I did not go back to prison, life on the street was still a struggle. I had to fight to stay on the right path. It often felt like an inner battle of two wills. I was in a place where I had to make some decisions. Do I try my luck at crime again, or do I stick to the original plan of being a law-abiding citizen? I had my grandmother in one ear saying, "Stay out of trouble and live right." Then I had so-called friends saying, "You ready to get back on your feet?" When I was in this struggle, I remembered the call home to my daughter from jail, and it made me choose to do the right thing. I was able to land a job with a security company, which was funny. Imagine coming from prison and landing a job enforcing the law!

I was working, life was good and I was starting to feel normal when I found out that while I was in prison, my grandmother had battled breast cancer. The pain I felt, knowing that she'd had to deal with that by herself while I was in prison made me cry. I know she was worried she could possibly die while I was in prison. This made me work harder to stay on the right path. I knew then that I wouldn't do anything to risk my freedom again, because she wouldn't be able to withstand a second bid.

The breast cancer would come back with a vengeance about four years later, landing her in hospice care. I quit my job to be my grandmother's caregiver. She lasted about a year; I was there when she took her last breath. She died while I was holding her hand, I told her how much I loved her and that she didn't have to hold on for me. I was going to be alright; she didn't need to worry about me.

God has blessed me to overcome trauma, violence, drug abuse, poverty, and prison, amongst other things. My journey has not been an easy journey, but I thank God that my grandmother raised me and for all her prayers, which still sustain me today. I continue to strive to do what's right, and I have seen God's blessings. It is so important to have a relationship with God and pray for His guidance in life.

ABOUT THE AUTHOR

Keenan Bishop is currently a professional bus operator in the greater Philadelphia transportation industry. Keenan's journey has not been an easy one, nonetheless, he has been able to overcome many of life's adversities because of his relationship with God and the prayers of his beloved grandmother.

Keenan's goal is to empower and give hope to young boys and men who have stories that are similar to his story. By speaking to and mentoring them, he seeks to deter them from a life of violence, drug use, and crime.

After spending time in SCI Albion State Prison on multiple offences, Keenan was granted a second chance. He has never looked back.

MESSAGE OF HOPE 7

ET TU, BRUTE?

DELVIA Y. BERRIAN

Trust in the LORD with all thine heart; and lean not unto thine own understanding. [6] In all thy ways acknowledge him, and he shall direct thy paths.

— Proverbs 3: 5–6

"Et tu, Brute" is a famous line quoted by Julius Caesar as he was being stabbed by his friend in a book by William Shakespeare's "The Tragedy of Julius Caesar." Jesus, just like Caesar, was betrayed and died at the hands of someone close to Him. Judas didn't participate in the crucifixion of Jesus, but his act of betrayal led to his death. Judas's role was very crucial in getting Jesus to the cross; the fifty pieces of silver Judas received helped save Christians. Jesus was the ultimate sacrifice, as His death provided redemption of sins as the sacrificial lamb.

Betrayal is defined by Merriam-Webster as violation of a person's trust or confidence, of a moral standard. Trust is very important in any relationship, and to betray someone's trust and confidence can sometimes be unrepairable. The betrayals of Jesus and Caesar led to their death. Caesar was unsuspecting of what was going to happen to him, but Jesus knew He was going to be sacrificed; He was fulfilling his purpose, His destiny, and the reason He was created.

Trust for me has always been an issue. Our family of origin is what shapes us and mold us as children. We often take those experiences into adulthood. We learn values, morals, and boundaries from our family system. These qualities do not necessarily have to be right in the eyes of society, but they are right in the eyes of the family. Broken trust coupled with sexual trauma made it very difficult for me to develop trusting relationships until I went through my healing process @Come Out of The Ashes. As my relationship with God deepened, I learned to trust Him with everything. I was able to develop trusting relationships with other people. Just like Jesus, I had a core group of people I allowed to experience my Garden of Gethsemane and Mountain of Transfiguration. There were two people I could say I told everything to and trusted with everything. They were to me what Peter, James, and John were to Jesus. I loved these people, and there was nothing I wouldn't do for them. Then I found out they were really my Judas. I don't believe the relationships started out as them having ill intentions, but I never stopped to reassess the relationships, nor did I pay attention to see if anything had changed in our interactions.

In retrospect, I know their season was over, but the damage that was caused from those experiences cut my soul. It was very damaging to have my trust violated after working so hard to learn to trust. I'd never experienced genuine love or acceptance. Coming from a place of self-destruction meant that developing authentic relationships with people was a big deal. What I learned from this experience was to monitor who I have close to me. As I prayed for God to help me not be vengeful and heal, the Lord kept repeating the scripture when Jesus elevated the disciples to apostles.

"I am sending you out like sheep among wolves. Therefore, be as shrewd as snakes and as innocent as doves."

— Matthew 10:16

I didn't understand why God kept repeating this scripture in my spirit, so I analyzed the animals in the scripture, as well as exegesis the text. I knew there was something I needed to learn from this experience, and God was giving me the key. As I looked at the text, the four animals stood out: sheep, wolves, snakes, and doves. Jesus often referred to his followers as sheep. Christians are considered sheep because we follow the shepherd, our pastor, or leaders. We are under their care and supervision, and they are to lead and guide us. He says He is sending us out like sheep amongst wolves. Most people believe sheep are dumb because it is the shepherd that guides them along the way. Then you have some that say sheep aren't dumb, but are blind. A sheep's pupils are actually rectangular, which gives them good peripheral vision; their field of vision is between 270 and 320 degrees, but the perception is bad. They can't see what's in front of them, but they can see the predator from far off. A sheep can't see what's right under their nose. I was really amazed at what I learned about the eyesight of the sheep and how it relates to interacting with people.

I then went on to look at the wolf. What I knew about wolves was that they were predators, but I wanted to learn more of their characteristics. Wolves are social animals, so family or pack is important, and hierarchy is important within the pack. Wolves are ambitious, and when I read that wolves preyed on injured animals, it was an *ah ha* moment for me. Wolves looked for weakness and zeroed in on that to get close.

God was saying, "I'm sending you, my child, out, even though you can't see what's in front of you in the midst of people who are going to prey on your weakness. But be wise as a serpent and gentle as a dove." This scripture was teaching me how to interact with people. The serpent represented power and protection of power, order, control, and ritualistic thinking and behavior. Snakes are solitary animals and are not aggressive. God is telling us that as sheep, we need to be knowledgeable, calculating, and intentional in our dealings with people, but gentle as a dove. Doves are a symbol of peace, so exhibiting a dove's personality is being an easygoing, friendly person and team player. Doves are tenderhearted, hardworking, and loyal. They avoid conflict.

As God kept repeating this scripture and the more, I learned about the characteristics of the animals, and learned how to move forward in dealing with people. But I was still stuck with this hurt where my reality and my expectations were clashing. How did I heal from this hurt? The setback was more devastating than I thought. Although God gave me the blueprint on how to move forward with people, any sign of familiarity was a flashback or setback in my thinking, and caused me to harden my heart. I had to ask myself, "How do I monitor people without being suspicious of every sign of change?" "How do I go on without becoming jaded and pushing people away?" It only could be done through prayer and trusting God. It took me a while to honestly forgive and recognize that I was still having residual effects from the bite. What helped me with this was a story about the Apostle Paul in Acts 28:3.

> *As Paul gathered an armful of sticks and was laying them on the fire, a poisonous snake, driven out by the heat, bit him on the hand. 4 The people of the island saw it hanging from his hand and said to each other, "A murderer, no doubt! Though he escaped the sea, justice will not permit him to live." 5 But Paul shook off the snake into the fire and was unharmed. 6 The*

people waited for him to swell up or suddenly drop dead. But when they had waited a long time and saw that he wasn't harmed, they changed their minds and decided he was a god.

Paul was bitten by the snake and shook it off. When we are bitten by a snake, betrayed by a friend, we must shake it off. The snake bite or betrayal was meant to stop you or cause you to die. People are going to be watching how you handle the bite, and some may even be waiting for you to die. We can't allow someone else's pain to hinder our progress towards our destiny. I had to be determined and intentional about my healing and being able to trust again. I did not want someone else's baggage to become my baggage.

God eventually uses the betrayal or hurt for our good. I know you're wondering how something painful or deceiving could be for our good. As I look back on every situation, I felt my trust was broken, but it worked out for my good. In Romans, the scripture tells us that God uses all things for our good; the good, the bad, and the very ugly will be used to fulfill God's purpose.

And we know that all things work together for good to them that love God, to them who are the called according to his purpose. For whom he did foreknow, he also did predestinate to be conformed to the image of his Son, that he might be the firstborn among many brethren. Moreover whom he did predestinate, them he also called: and whom he called, them he also justified: and whom he justified, them he also glorified. What shall we then say to these things? If God be for us, who can be against us?

Remembering that if God be for us, nothing anyone can do will harm us. It may hurt temporarily, but if we stick with God, it will eventually prove to have been less than God's best. I spoke earlier of the two friends I had that were important in my life. One was a male that I was romantically involved with. For 2 ½ years, I was at this man's beck and call, showing him I was an exceptional woman. I allowed him to use me and treat me in any kind of way, because I thought this was a good thing that God had allowed into my life. Again, his treatment reflected how I saw myself. Honestly, no matter how good of a person he was, he was not a God thing. He was one of the few men I dated who had his own things and was self-sufficient, and that was probably why I thought he was a good thing. But in the end, it turned out to be a damaging relationship for my heart and soul.

As I analyzed the relationship, I began to feel sorry for him, because he only projected the pain he felt onto me: the failure to develop a deep relationship with anyone, afraid to take a chance on love, unable to let go of past hurt caused by his ex-wife, and unwillingness to trust anyone. After the breakdown of our friendship/relationship, I developed those same characteristics and became unwilling to develop any trusting relationships. Unlike this person, I made a conscious decision to heal from that wrong touch or interaction. It became a continuous effort on my part to develop deep relationships, trust people, allow someone to love me, and realize that I was deserving of love.

One of the revelations the Lord gave me concerning the place I was in with relationships came from a recent parasailing experience. I was very scared to try parasailing, but I went along with it anyway, trusting that God was in control. As I experienced the parasailing, I prayed, cried, and screamed, but I did it. During the parasailing experience, I did not let what I saw affect my ability to trust that God would bring me through. The wind was raging, and my environment was very unstable and unfamiliar, but I had faith that God would not allow me to be hurt. This was the approach I needed to stretch in my area of fear with relationships.

How do you overcome an act of betrayal or broken trust? You must trust God! Trusting God is knowing God's heart toward you. It is also going on your knowledge of God and His track record with you. Many times, we are put in situations that challenge what we know about God, but it will increase our faith. It depends on how you look at your situation. Are you looking at it as a King's kid, a child of God? As a King's kid, you know you are the apple of God's eye. Scripture tells us how God loves and protects us in Deuteronomy 32:10. "In a desert land he found him, in a barren and howling waste. He shielded him and cared for him; he guarded him as the apple of his eye, like an eagle that stirs up its nest and hovers over its young, that spreads its wings to catch them and carries them aloft."

There is scripture after scripture telling of God's love, His plans, and how He feels toward his children. Scripture says in Jeremiah 29:11 "For I know the plans I have declares the Lord, plans to prosper you and not to harm you, plans to give you a hope and a future." Are you looking at what you see in the natural, instead of what you know about God? Satan attacks us in what we know about God. He attempts to discredit God based on what you see. In Matthew 14, we see how we must trust God even in tumultuous situations. Jesus sends the disciples out to sea after feeding five thousand as they were out to sea, the winds were raging.

Shortly before dawn Jesus went out to them, walking on the lake. When the disciples saw him walking on the lake, they were terrified. "It's a ghost," they said, and cried out in fear. 27 But Jesus immediately said to them: "Take courage! It is I. Don't be afraid." "Lord, if it's you," Peter replied, "tell me to come to you on the water." "Come," he said. Then Peter got down out of the boat, walked on the water, and came toward Jesus. But when he saw the wind, he was afraid and, beginning to sink, cried out, "Lord, save me!" Immediately Jesus reached out his hand and caught him. "You of little faith," he said, "why did you doubt?" In this scripture we see how Peter was more worried about the natural and what he saw instead of what he knew about Jesus. Peter was there with Jesus as he performed miracle after miracle; so why would he doubt that he would be safe.

I can think of countless times God has proven to be faithful, but there have been times I have doubted God because I was focused on what was in front of me and not on my experience. *It used to take me a while to get focused, and sometimes may take a while for me to get to a place to recall God's faithfulness.* I learned to rely on God based on my experience with Him. When in doubt or uncertain, I pull out my stone of Ebenezer, when God showed himself faithful. I learned reading a story of Samuel, in 1 Samuel 7, that we should have a stone of Ebenezer when God defeats our enemy or shows Himself faithful. In this story, the Israelites were afraid because they were being pursued by the Philistines. They sought the assistance of the prophet Samuel, who instructed them to turn from their foreign gods and commit themselves to the Lord and serve Him only, and He would deliver them out of the hand of the Philistines.

As the Israelites were fasting and praying, the Philistines devised a plan to attack them. The Israelites, under the instruction of Samuel, continued to cry out to God, who caused the Philistines to be put in a state of confusion, which allowed the Israelites to defeat them. "Then Samuel took a stone and set it up between Mizpah and Shen. He named it Ebenezer, saying, 'Thus far the Lord has helped us.'" The stone of Ebenezer signifies that trusting in anything or anyone short of Christ is a precursor to failure. Remember that the stone of Ebenezer is a stone of help, a place of victory, and a place of assurance that God has your back.

I have countless stories of how God was with me in places of hurt, pain, or disappointment. There were times I prayed for things and really needed those things to manifest in my life, but God either didn't allow them to happen, or He made me wait. As I reflect on those experiences, I see how God worked them out for my good.

I remember when my oldest daughter was about three months old and the Philadelphia Housing Authority was accepting applications for people with one child. I stood in this very long line to submit my application, and was very hopeful because I really needed to have my own place. I met the criteria, I was low income and had one child. I remember fantasizing about having my own place and how it would be a relief not to worry about my home life. When I got the denial letter, I was devastated. I cried out to God, because He knew my living situation was not the best. I didn't understand why He didn't allow me to get low-income housing.

Today, I can look back and say God had better for me. I am a homeowner. I am not sure what God was protecting me from, because the housing was in a drug-infested violent neighborhood. Who knows, I may have gotten comfortable living with less than God's best for myself. I may not have accomplished what I have thus far if I lived there; only God knows. My simple drug use could have turned into a bigger problem. I have countless stories of how something, someone, or some situation I wanted where God said no or wait and it turned out to be much better than I expected or anticipated.

As I was writing this chapter, the Lord brought to my remembrance a time when I broke a friend's trust. When I think about what happened, I see that my actions were selfish, and there's nothing else to say about it. My actions didn't harm her physically, but they hurt her feelings. Her feelings did not matter to me at the time, because I felt she did not deserve the opportunity at hand. I know this is too deep and transparent for some people, but it's true. I deserved this opportunity, because I was better prepared to take advantage of the opportunity. When I analyze how I was thinking back then, I feel ashamed and I believe the Lord brought this to my remembrance not to bring about shame, but for me to have grace toward the two people who betrayed *my* trust. Not that we will reconcile and be friends as we were previously, but for me to extend the same grace God extended toward me. I have forgiven them, I recognize why the relationships had to end, and God has blessed me with new core friends.

In each and in every situation, we must trust God with all our hearts and lean not to our own understanding but in all our ways acknowledge Him and He will direct our paths. If I can keep this in the forefront of my mind when dealing with people, situations, and circumstances, it will give me the peace and security to remember that God is in control.

ABOUT THE LEAD AUTHOR

Delvia Y. Berrian is a native of Philadelphia, Pennsylvania. She is a graduate of Temple University College of Public Health School of Social Work. She earned her Bachelor's and Master's degrees in Social Work. She also earned a Master's degree in Theological Studies from Palmer Theological Seminary.

Delvia has served as a child welfare advocate for nearly three decades.

Delvia is a woman after God's heart. She is known for her many acts of kindness and for her dedication to improving the lives of children and youth. It has always been her passion to inspire women and girls to strive to reach their greatest potential.

Delvia is the author of *Beauty for Ashes: Freedom from the Wrong Touch*. She is also the founder of PRESS for Kingdom Living, an organization committed to empowering young girls and women. Her goal is support them by offering workshops, coaching and other events that help them to live God-fearing lives, while overcoming life's challenges. Ultimately, she wants to see women catapulted into their God-given purposes.

Made in the USA
Middletown, DE
25 May 2021